THE CAPITOLINE
MUSEUMS

Comune di Roma
Assessorato alle Politiche Culturali

Sovraintendenza ai Beni Culturali

THE CAPITOLINE MUSEUMS

 Electa

The Capitoline Museums
April 18, 2000

Comune di Roma
Assessorato alle Politiche Culturali

Gianni Borgna
Assessore

Sovraintendenza ai Beni Culturali

Eugenio La Rocca
Sovraintendente

Anna Mura Sommella
Dirigente dei Musei di Arte Antica

Maria Elisa Tittoni
*Dirigente dei Musei di Arte Medioevale
e Moderna*

Texts
Margherita Albertoni, Maddalena Cima,
Maria Dell'Era, Sergio Guarino,
Patrizia Masini, Marina Mattei,
Anna Mura Sommella, Micaela Perrone,
Emilia Talamo

Photographs
Archives of the Capitoline Museums

Translation by
Darius A. Arya and Silvia Mari

Cover
Group of Commodus as Hercules
flanked by two Tritons.
Palazzo dei Conservatori, Hall of the Tapestries

Table of Contents

The Capitoline Hill

Walking up the monumental ramp (*cordonata*), one comes upon the piazza
of the Capitoline Hill (*Campidoglio*), a remarkable architectural project
designed by Michelangelo. This space also represents the outcome of a history
spanning 1000 years, which singled out the Capitoline Hill as the religious
and political center of the city.

In the beginning a small, central valley characterized the hill and divided two
wooded rises, the *Arx* and *Capitolium*. Legendary tradition locates in this valley
the mythic *Asylum*, instituted by Romulus for gathering the inhabitants from
nearby populations. Today, in light of archaeological research conducted
(and still in progress) in the area comprised by the Palazzo dei Conservatori
(Palace of the Conservators), the legendary stories handed down concerning
the origins of the city appear scientifically more documentable and closer
to historical reality than ever. In fact, the archaeological strata regarding the most
ancient phase of the Capitoline Hill show traces of inhabitation on the hill,
beginning at the end of the Bronze Age (1200-1000 BC). These important
archaeological studies (still in the preliminary stages) recognize faint traces
of a settlement. Some burials of children and the remains of the widespread
production of metal-based handcrafts belong to the site.

In the historical period, the Capitoline Hill appeared as the one and only sacred
acropolis of the city. The last kings of the Roman tradition, the Tarquins, built
the Temple of Capitoline Jupiter on the *Capitolium*. However, the temple was not
dedicated until the first year of the Republican era, 509 BC. The temple became
the symbol of Roman civilization, replicated in all of the new cities founded
by Rome. It was the destination of the triumphal ceremonies held in honor
of victorious generals upon their return to Rome. The long triumphal procession
winded through the city, exhibiting prisoners and spoils of war along
the Via Sacra and up to the Temple of Jupiter, in whose name campaigns
of conquest were undertaken. Recent archaeological surveys have revealed
the imposing foundations of the temple, perfectly preserved and incorporated
into the structures of the sixteenth century Palazzo Caffarelli. The Temple
of Juno Moneta, site of the mint of the Roman State, stood on the *Arx*, the rise
that tradition assigned to the Sabine population and on which today stands
the impressive structure of the Basilica of the Aracoeli.

At the end of the Republican period, the construction of massive structures

of the *Tabularium*, which housed the Archives of the Roman State, regularized
the slopes of the Capitoline Hill facing the Forum. The imposing building did
not alter the preexisting Temple of Jupiter Veiovis (196 BC), characterized
by a transverse axis. The mysterious divinity related to Jupiter and the underworld
was the recipient of the cult. Many other temples on the Capitoline affirmed
the sacredness of the hill.

In the Republican period the construction of public buildings shows
the competition for supremacy that existed among the most important noble
Roman families. Beyond the Temple of Capitoline Jupiter, the ancient sources
attest to the existence of other sanctuaries in the area dedicated to *Jupiter
Feretrius, Fides, Mens, Venus Erycina, Ops, Jupiter Tonans, Mars Ultor*,
and *Jupiter Custos*. In the mediaeval period, the ancient buildings fell into disuse,
but the memory of the ancient greatness was recorded in the description
of the *Mirabilia*: "*Capitolium* is thus named because it was the head of the entire
world and because Consuls and Senators lived there in order to govern the city
and the world. High, solid walls entirely encrusted with glass and gold
and marvelously engraved works protected its face. At the center of the citadel
rose a palace, entirely decorated with gold and precious stones, that seems
to have been worth one third of the entire world [...]."

Anonymous drawing from
the middle of the sixteenth
century, the Capitoline "plain"

The Corsi family transformed the structures of the *Tabularium* into a stronghold.
First Henry IV (1084) then Pasquale II (1105) chased away the Corsi family
in order to prevent a dangerous, alternative center of power from forming there.
In 1130, through the decree of Anacletus II, the Benedictines of the Aracoeli
became the proprietors of the Capitoline Hill. During the entire mediaeval
period, the architectural history of the Capitoline Hill overlapped with the
vicissitudes of the municipal institutions. In 1143/1144 – the year of the birth
of the Municipality of Rome – an antipapal revolution (*renovatio Senatus*) installed
on the Capitoline Hill a collegial magistracy composed of fifty Senators invested
with public and judicial functions. At the beginning of the thirteenth century
the magistracy that was composed of one or two Senators, assisted by a Municipal
Board with deliberative power, substituted the collegial magistracy. In 1299,
the opening of a loggia (covered terrace) facing the piazza that hosted the market
transformed the Palazzo Senatorio. This action thus confirmed the overturning
of the topographical situation; whereas in the Roman period, the principal
monuments on the hill faced the monumental center of the city (i.e., towards the
Forum), in the mediaeval period the Capitoline Hill faced the Campus Martius.
In 1363, the first public statutes defined the form of government chosen
by the city, i.e., a single foreign Senator assisted by three elected magistrates,
the Conservators, representatives of the new social classes in power.
In the fifteenth century, Palazzo Senatorio appeared as a fortress with towers,
constructed by Boniface IX (1389-1404), Martin V (1427), and Nicholas V
(1447-1455). The palace façade, with a double staircase, facing the piazza had
three Guelph-cross windows and a loggia on the second floor. This period also
witnessed the transformation of the palace of the Banderesi (i.e., Captains of the
public *militia*) into the monumental premises of the Conservators. Documents
of the fifteenth century attribute this construction to Nicholas V. Cohabitation
between the municipal institutions and the papacy was not always peaceful.
In the meanwhile, the distinction between the Capitoline Hill as a place
of memory and Vatican as a place of the pontifical power became clear. In 1471,
Sixtus IV ennobled the function of the Capitoline Hill through a donation
to the People of Rome. He gave large bronze statues that had been housed
in the patriarch's Lateran residence. This act brought about the creation
of the oldest public museum in the world. The She-wolf, placed on the façade

of the Palazzo dei Conservatori, became the symbol of the city. The colossal
bronze portrait of Constantine with the *"palla Sansonis"* was placed in the
external portico.

Architecturally, the Capitoline piazza remained virtually unchanged until 1537.
In this year, Paul III Farnese commissioned Michelangelo to transfer
the equestrian statue of Marcus Aurelius from the Lateran to the Capitoline
and to systematize it in the center of the piazza. The statue had escaped the
normal fate of ancient bronze statues because in the mediaeval period it was
believed that it represented Constantine, the first Christian emperor. The papal
project, fiercely opposed by the Lateran canons and, it seems, Michelangelo
himself, was completed in the following year. The presence and the strong visual
effect of the statue, extraordinarily charged with symbolic significance
and historical importance, created a new fulcrum at the center of the piazza
and forever changed the aspect of the Capitoline piazza.

The pope entrusted the systematization of the area to the ingenious
Michelangelo. Plans, probably under way during the period of the transfer
of the colossal bronze statue of Marcus Aurelius, took shape in the following
decades. The project was not finished until more than a century later, with
the completion of the Palazzo Nuovo (New Palace). Renovation began with
the Palazzo Senatorio. The palace preserves, within its structure, the ancient
remains of the *Tabularium*, and mediaeval and Renaissance period structures,
all of which symbolize its uninterrupted building phases. An imposing façade
transformed the palace on the side facing the square. Large-scale pilasters
and a double monumental staircase divided the façade. The staircase gave access
to the "noble floor," which earlier had housed a loggia and the hall of the Senator.
Then, the installation of a fountain enriched the façade. In addition, colossal
statues representing Rivers, found at the beginning of the century on the
Quirinal, flanked the fountain. Since 1513 the statues, depicted in a lying pose,
had been arranged on the square to face the façade of the Palazzo dei
Conservatori. Finally, in a niche at the center of the façade, came the addition
of an ancient porphyry statue of seated Minerva, transformed into the goddess
Roma through the addition of attributes typical of the deity. Thus, the decorative
program was complete in 1588.

The transformation of the Palazzo dei Conservatori began in 1563, under the

Jeronymus Cock,
the Capitoline piazza (1562)

pontificate of Pius IV. A long portico with colonnaded arcades characterized
the original façade. The presence of two of the most prestigious works from
the Capitoline collections, the She-wolf and the colossal bronze head
of Constantine, distinguished the façade. The She-wolf replaced the lion as the
civic symbol of the city. In the mediaeval period first it was located in front of the
Palazzo Senatorio and then was moved inside "in a covered loggia overlooking
the city plain" (Aldrovandi). The addition of a pair of twins transformed the statue
from a symbol of justice, while in the Lateran, to *Mater Romanorum*. The colossal
head was relocated to the courtyard, where the number of monuments increased
year after year to enrich the Capitoline collections of antiquity. The project
of Michelangelo was completed only after his death. This project strengthened
the fifteenth century structure of the palace through a geometrical design, which

was articulated by a large-scale order of Corinthian pilasters recalling the pattern of the Palazzo Senatorio. The plan also regularized the form of the courtyard and inserted, within the building, a large, monumental staircase, to reach the upper story. This staircase replaced an external staircase in the courtyard, visible in some ancient drawings. In addition, in some parts, it modified the internal layout of rooms. A well-balanced, extraordinary urban plan took into account the slightly deviating course of the structure of the palace in relation to the façade of Palazzo Senatorio and in respect to the central axis of the piazza, marked by the equestrian statue of Marcus Aurelius. This divergent course suggested that the architectural design of the piazza needed to be completed by the construction of a twin palace on the opposite side. This new palace had to be equally divergent in such a way as to accompany the gaze of one who ascended the redesigned monumental ramp (*cordonata*) originating from the Campus Martius towards the Palazzo Senatorio.

A series of engravings (dating to 1567-1569) by Etienne Dupérac attest to the conception of the project, which found its logical conclusion only through the construction of the Palazzo Nuovo. Until that time a large retaining wall for the enormous Basilica of the Aracoeli delimited the left side of the piazza. In 1596, according to the drawing of Giacomo della Porta, the installation of the impressive fountain of the Marforio decorated this side of the piazza. However, construction of the structure began only in 1603, under the pontificate of Clement VIII. With little variation the building adhered to the original design conceived by Michelangelo. In 1667, after difficult building episodes, Pope Alexander VII oversaw the completion of the building. However, the new museum, destined to house the Capitoline collections of antiquity, was not dedicated until 1734 (the pontificate of Clement XII).

In this period, the piazza of the Capitoline Hill reached its definitive configuration. Two colossal statues of the Dioscouri, found in the vicinity of the Ghetto, the imposing "Trophies of Marius," removed from the large, monumental fountain on the Esquiline, and the statues of Constantine and his son Constantine II, transferred from the Aracoeli, enriched the balustrade that faced the Campus Martius. The precious star-shaped pavement design was the last element required for the completion of the project designed by Michelangelo. Although not constructed until 1940, it appears in Dupérac's

Palazzo dei Conservatori,
Hall of the Eagles:
representation
of games conducted
on the Capitoline piazza

engravings. The isolation of the entire Capitoline Hill and the large-scale
intervention that created a large subterranean gallery to join the three palaces
facing the piazza provided an opportunity to install the pavement inspired by,
although not perfectly adherent to, Michelangelo's design. Construction
of the pavement closed the chapter on the creation of a single architectural space
that was fully coherent and "perfect," after centuries of elaboration
and adjustments. It is for this reason that the Capitoline Hill represents a museum
complex of extraordinary historical and cultural significance. The piazza,
the palaces, the archaeological and historical-artistic collections, and now, with
the reopening of the subterranean gallery, also the principal ancient monuments
constitute organic and harmonious elements of the museum complex.

Beginning in the fifteenth century, the formation of the Capitoline Museums of antiquity was characterized by new interest in the archaeological patrimony of ancient Rome as the object of antiquarianism and collecting, rather than the object of potential reuse.

In 1471, Pope Sixtus IV donated four very famous bronze sculptures – the She-Wolf, the *Spinario* (boy pulling a thorn out of his foot), the Camillus, and the bronze head of Constantine with hand and globe – until that moment exhibited in front of the patriarch's Lateran residence. Because of their location in the Lateran, they symbolized the continuity between imperial Rome and the temporal power of the Church. The donation marks the beginning of the return of ancient sculptural works to the Capitoline Hill and the birth of the Capitoline museum complex.

In fact, centuries of devastation and abandonment, followed by the collapse of the Roman empire, had despoiled the hill of temples, honorary arches, and statues that had rendered famous the *Capitolium fulgens*, recorded with amazement by Roman authors of the late-antique period.

The works constituted the *thesaurus Romanitatis*, a sort of inheritance from the ancient world that the Church had collected and jealously guarded during the entire mediaeval period. Through this strongly symbolic gesture, the works returned to the People of Rome to be located on the hill representative of Rome's sacred past.

A long inscription, still preserved to this day and located at the entrance of the Palazzo dei Conservatori, records the details of this event. The inscription documents the important moment of the creation of the Capitoline museum complex, by citing the generous donation that, *"ob immensam benignitatem,"* Sixtus IV gave to the People of Rome.

The text indicates wisely that this was not a simple donation but, rather, a true "restitution" of the remarkable works of bronze, testimony of the ancient magnificence of the People of Rome who had created them: *"Aeneas insignes statuas – priscae excellentiae virtutisque monumentum – Romano populo unde exorte fuere restituendas condonandasque censuit."* Sixtus IV's precious gift clearly was intended to confirm the predominance of the pontifical power on the Capitoline Hill, through the consecration of this ancient hill as an important symbol of ancient Rome.

This act contrasted with the role attributed to the Capitoline Hill as the central
proponent of civic independence, tenaciously defended by the magistracy
of the Capitoline.
In this way, began a confrontation (utilizing symbolic language) between
the papal power and the Municipality of Rome. This confrontation brought
about, in the span of a century, the total transformation of the Capitoline piazza.
Two sixteenth century views, one, a drawing by M. van Heemskerck,
and the other, a fresco in the Hall of the Eagles in the Palazzo dei Conservatori,
document with great accuracy the condition of the Capitoline area during
the first half of the sixteenth century. At this time, the mediaeval configuration
still characterized the area. In addition, the small fresco attests to the beginning
of the process of transformation, determined by the transfer of the equestrian
statue of Marcus Aurelius from the Lateran in 1538.
The statue became the focal point of the architectural systematization
of the piazza, according to the will of Paul III and designed by Michelangelo.
The statuary group of "A lion attacking a horse" appears in the drawing
of Heemskerck, only a few years older than the fresco, in its mediaeval location,
at the top of the stairs of access to the Palazzo Senatorio.

Palazzo dei Conservatori,
Hall of the Eagles:
the Capitoline piazza

This work, the symbol of juridical power Senate's authority, was the only
ancient sculpture present on the Capitoline Hill before the Sixtus IV's
donation. The statue characterized the *locus iustitiae*, already recorded
in fourteenth century documents, where it was common to pronounce and,
sometimes carry out, capital sentences.

With the systematization of the façade of Palazzo Senatorio, on the occasion
of the monumental transformation of the Capitoline piazza, this statue group
became part of the Capitoline collections of antiquity.

In the same drawing, in addition to the bronze head of Constantine located
within the arcades, the statue of the She-wolf appears on the façade
of the Palazzo dei Conservatori, transferred according to the will of Sixtus IV
from the *campus Lateranensis*. Before 1509, an anonymous artist added
the figures of the twins. This intervention definitively cancelled the ominous
characteristic of the symbol of justice that the She-wolf had had in the Lateran,
and, instead, underlined the symbol of *Mater Romanorum*, more appropriate
for a work that already had become the emblem of the municipality's power.

In the period between the date of the drawing (1532-1537) and that of the fresco
(1541-1543), the She-wolf was transferred inside the palace "*in porticu interiori*

Marten van Heemskerck,
detail of the view
of the Capitoline Hill
with the statue of a River god
in front of the portico
of the Palazzo dei Conservatori

prope aulam," i.e., in the portico located on the far right of the palace, next
to the main room now called the hall "of the Horatii and Curiatii."
Important works of ancient sculpture reached the Capitoline Hill between
the end of the fifteenth century and the first half of the sixteenth century,
creating a remarkable collection in front of the Palazzo dei Conservatori.
This antiquarian patrimony of enormous historical and artistic value confirmed
the role of the Capitoline as a public museum of antiquity. The Conservators
purchased the bronze statue of Hercules found in the Forum Boarium during
the papacy of Sixtus IV. The statue played a very important role among
the first works of art destined to augment the original nucleus of bronze
statues donated by Sixtus IV. The Conservators displayed the statue on a high
base in front of their palace, as a "monument of the glory of Rome."
This statue is a copy of a Greek original dating to the fourth century BC.
It was successively moved first to the courtyard, where Heemskerck saw it,
and then transferred inside the palace, into the Apartment of the Conservators
(cf. U. Aldrovandi, *Delle statue antiche che per tutta Roma in diversi luoghi
e case si veggono*, Venezia 1556, p. 273).
In 1513, two colossal statues of river divinities, found in the Baths of Constantine
on the Quirinal, were placed on either side of the entrance of the palace.
In 1588-1589, these sculptures, dating to the Trajanic period, constituted
part of the sculptural group located on the monumental staircase that acts
as an entrance to the Palazzo Senatorio.
A little while later (1515) came the acquisition of the three large, high relief
panels decorated with scenes related to the life of Marcus Aurelius.
They originally pertained to the sculptural decoration that adorned a
monument celebrating the emperor on the occasion of his triumph in AD 176.
These reliefs signify one of the highest expressions of sculpture of historical
character that Roman art has passed down to us. They represent the
submission of the barbarians, the triumph, and sacrifice before the Temple
of Capitoline Jupiter. In addition, the reliefs are documents of exceptional
value destined to represent the ideal continuity between the ancient world
and the Renaissance-period Capitoline Hill.
At the beginning of the sixteenth century, thanks to the works of F. Albertini,
Opusculum de Mirabilibus, in 1510, and Fulvio, *Antiquaria Urbis*, in 1513,

Stefano della Bella,
the Courtyard of the Palazzo
dei Conservatori

we know with sufficient precision the display of the Capitoline collections.
In fact, we know that at the beginning of the sixteenth century a great part
of the sculptures were arranged within the Palazzo dei Conservatori, whereas
the large-scale statues were located in the courtyard of the same building.
The courtyard, which today we see in its eighteenth century phase, has been
modified in respect to the Renaissance phase through the addition of a portico
along the wall facing the entrance. The so-called "Cesi Roma" and the statues
of the barbarians in *bigio* marble were located in the portico. On the right side
of the courtyard, stood the Hercules from the Forum Boarium and the remains
of the great acrolith of Constantine from the Basilica of Maxentius. On the left
side, stood the three reliefs of Marcus Aurelius, which Leo X transferred from

Courtyard of the Palazzo
dei Conservatori with
the fragments of the colossal
statue of Constantine

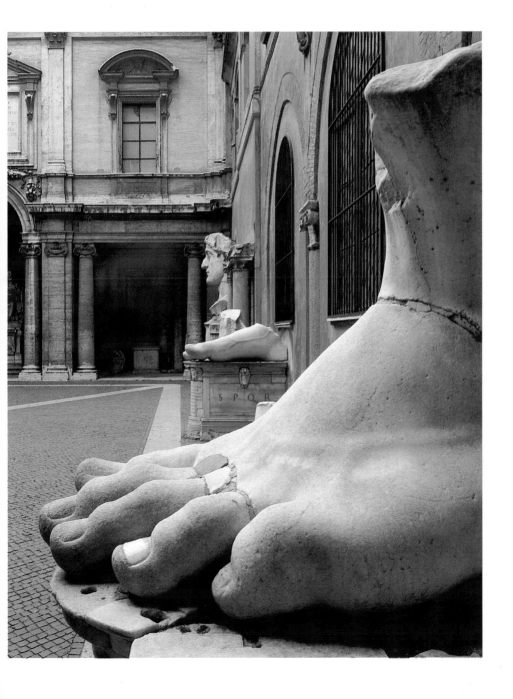

the Church of Santi Luca e Martina in the Roman Forum. In 1594, the head
of the acrolith of Constantine was transferred to the pediment located over
the fountain of Marforio, as decoration of the retaining wall of the Church
of the Aracoeli.

A drawing by Stefano della Bella attests that the colossal head returned
definitively to the Courtyard of the Palazzo dei Conservatori in 1659.
In 1541, a colossal statue of Athena, found and donated to the city magistracy
during the papacy of Paul III, occupied a niche in front of the entrance,
on the central axis of the courtyard. Shortly thereafter (under the papacy
of Sixtus V), the statue became the center of a lively *querelle* (controversy)
when it was used as a central element in the decoration of the large staircase
designed by Michelangelo for the Palazzo Senatorio. The over life-sized
sculpture had been removed already from the back wall of the courtyard
to permit the installation of the *Fasti Consolari* fragments. The fragments
came to light in the Roman Forum in 1546. A few years later, Cardinal
Farnese donated them to the People of Rome. Onofrio Panvinio records that
Michelangelo himself assisted in the recomposition and architectural
arrangement of the recovered fragments at the Capitoline. The *Fasti*
of the Capitoline, transferred in 1586 to the Hall of the She-wolf
(where they remain today), were reassembled according to Michelangelo's
design. However, during this systematization, major readjustments modified
his overall plan.

Available documentation regarding the oldest account of the collection describes
the situation of the Capitoline collections on the eve of two extraordinary events,
which determined a radical transformation of the collections. First, in 1563,
work began on the restructuring of the Palazzo dei Conservatori and the
subsequent resystematization of the works of art housed within the palace.
Second, in 1566, Pius V donated works of art to the People of Rome with
the intention of "purging the Vatican of pagan idols." Initially, the pope had
intended to donate 150 statues from the Vatican collections, but he substantially
revised his plan. Nevertheless, a considerable number of works, originally
housed in the Theater of the Belvedere, reached the Capitoline Hill
and enriched the "statuary collection," subsequently housed on the ground
floor of the Palazzo dei Conservatori.

Palazzo dei Conservatori,
Hall of the She-wolf

In addition, according to the engravings of Dupérac, some statues were
displayed on the old bell tower and on the façade of the Palazzo Senatorio,
in accordance with Michelangelo's design.
Restructuring of the Palazzo dei Conservatori finally permitted a suitable
arrangement of the works already in the Capitoline collection and other works
subsequently donated or purchased. Sculptures of great prestige became
part of the collections in the second half of the sixteenth century.
Among these are the two statues of Julius Caesar and Navarca, the Capitoline
Brutus, and the *Lex de imperio Vespasiani*. In 1568 the Hall of the
Horatii and Curiatii housed this extraordinary relic and the hand and globe

of Constantine (originally located in the external portico of the palace).
The entirely restructured courtyard housed the large sarcophagus of Alexander
Severus, acquired in 1590, and the statue group of "A lion attacking a horse"
(restored on this occasion by Ruggero Bescapè).
After the completion of the renovations in the Palazzo dei Conservatori,
the Marcus Aurelius reliefs went to a new location; they became immured
on the second floor landing of the staircase, where they are located to this day.
Many years later, the two colossal statues of the Dioscouri, found in 1560,
were placed on the balustrade that encloses the piazza. The erection
of the statues on their respective pedestals was very difficult because of their
fragmentary state. Indeed, a demanding restoration of the statues, initiated
in 1582, lasted several years. In 1590, under the papacy of Sixtus V,
the so-called "Trophies of Marius" were transferred to the Capitoline
to embellish the balustrade that encloses the piazza on the end facing the large
ramp (cordonata). In antiquity the "Trophies" had decorated the monumental
fountain created by Alexander Severus on the Esquiline. In 1590 as well,
two Egyptian lions were placed on the foot of the ramp.
Michaelis reports that, "the seventeenth century was as unproductive, regarding
the augmentation of the collection, as the sixteenth century was productive."
In fact, diffuse private collections and the birth of the great collections of
patrician palaces absorbed the best finds available on the antiquarian market.
A drawing by Stefano della Bella, completed after 1659, gives an idea of the
overcrowding condition characterizing the courtyard. Likewise, the Palazzo
dei Conservatori was so full of statues that it was very difficult for the ancient
civic magistracy, which utilized these spaces as an official and representative
seat, to execute its functions.
In 1603 construction of the Palazzo Nuovo on the left side of the square began
under Pope Clement VIII. Fifty years later, Carlo Rainaldi finally completed
the palace. Palazzo Nuovo became a museum only in 1733, when Clement XII
purchased the Albani Collection. In the preceding decades, this building
already hosted conspicuous numbers of statues that had originated
in the Palazzo dei Conservatori. The Palazzo Nuovo housed this collection
and the principal nucleus of the Albani Collection, which was characterized
by an exceptional compilation of portraits of famous men, philosophers,

Colossal statue
of one of the Dioscouri
on the balustrade
of the Capitoline piazza

and emperors. In 1734, immediately after the dedication of the museum,
Clement XII and Benedict XIV gave further donations. Numerous works
of art, including the *Dying Gaul* (1734), the *Satyr* in *rosso antico* marble
(1746), the group of *Amor and Psyche* and, finally, the famous *Capitoline
Venus* (1750) already in private collections or recently discovered, eventually
enriched the rooms decorated with the crests of Innocent X and Alexander
VII. In 1744, Benedict XIV donated the marble *Forma Urbis*, created
in the Severan period. It was arranged in 26 panels along the large staircase
that ascended to the first floor of the museum.

This exceptional historical-topographical document, discovered two centuries
before near the Church of Santi Cosma e Damiano, remained in the Capitoline
Museum until the beginning of the twentieth century. The two Centaurs
in *bigio morato*, arranged at the center of the Great Hall, and the very refined
Mosaic of the Doves, number among the most recent precious acquisitions
of the Museum.

All of them were found in the villa of the Emperor Hadrian in Tivoli.
Clement XIII donated them in the second half of the eighteenth century.
The Capitoline Museum represents a remarkable testimony of eighteenth
century museum display whose original context has remained intact.

The almost unaltered state of the eighteenth century Museum is perceptible
through a comparison between the rooms and the drawings of the rooms
executed in the eighteenth and nineteenth centuries. The engraving
of Natoire (1759), depicting the lobby of the museum and the courtyard,
records the fountain of the Marforio in its new eighteenth century location.
The lithograph of Benoist (1870) depicts the gilded bronze statue
of Hercules, previously located in the courtyard of Palazzo dei Conservatori,
in the area facing the Gallery.

The original arrangement of the works of art into categories and particular
criteria necessitated by restoration determined the layout of the works
within the rooms. In addition, the reconstruction and the interpretation
of the ancient sculpture highlight the particular character of the collection
as a testimony of the learned collecting that took place over the past centuries.
In 1771, the dedication of the Pius-Clement Museum in the Vatican marked
a static moment in the efforts to augment the archaeological collections in the

Capitoline. In fact, the popes paid singular attention, from that moment on, to the new museum. The situation became dramatic for the museum complex of the Capitoline when, as a result of the Treaty of Tolentino in 1797, many of the most famous works from the civic collections were transferred to France. After the fall of Napoleon, in 1815, only the tenacious intervention of Canova brought back the principal works of art to Italy. In this way, the *Spinario*, *Brutus*, *Capitoline Venus*, and the *Dying Gaul* were able to return to their original locations.

In 1838, according to the will of Gregory XVI, the civic magistracy regained the Capitoline Museum. However, simultaneously it was deprived of the rich collection of Egyptian sculptures. In exchange, it gained some works, including the Amendola sarcophagus and the Velletri-type Athena.

The acquisitions made in the first seventy years of the nineteenth century were few but significant. Particularly relevant is the group of large bronzes found in Vicolo delle Palme in Trastevere (1848), the collection of Greek and Etruscan vases donated by Augusto Castellani and especially the collection of ancient coins that eventually constituted the principal nucleus of the Capitoline Medal Collection. The year 1870 marked the transfer of the capital of the new Reign of Italy to Rome, and the vicissitudes at the end of the nineteenth century marked a fundamental milestone in the life and development of the city.

The transformation and enlargement of the Capitoline museum complex reflected the events in a very obvious manner. In fact, even the arrangement of the archaeological collections, located in the Palazzo Nuovo (the repository of a large collection of ancient sculpture), underwent a profound change. Indeed, the formulation of scientific criteria (made possible by the relevant contribution of material found during the excavations in the urban environment) substituted the prevalent antiquarian character of the collections formed through donations and acquisitions. The new political class generated feverish building activity and related excavation works in vast areas of the periphery in order to bestow the capital with public buildings and residential quarters due to new exigencies.

In fact, this agenda brought to light an enormous amount of archaeological material. In this way, a new section of the museum in the Palazzo dei Conservatori

developed. The palace lost its function as the official seat of the homonymous civic magistracy. In addition, it had enough room to house a wooden pavilion for a temporary presentation of the works of art found during the great excavations conducted in the urban surroundings.

In 1903, Rodolfo Lanciani oversaw the enlargement and new systematization of this sector of the Museum of the Palazzo dei Conservatori. He made it possible to obtain a better organization of the material according to new museological criteria, aimed at underlying the importance of the data obtained from excavations. Therefore, the works were distributed in the rooms according to their provenience, privileging a more articulated interpretation of the archaeological data rather than an "antiquarian" vision that tended to underline the aesthetic value of the sculptures as masterpieces of the ancient art.

The years of the Governorship, in particular between 1925 and 1930, witnessed a profound renewal of the Capitoline museum structures. The change ushered in the creation of a new museum section through the acquisition of Palazzo Caffarelli, previously owned by the Austrians. Sculptural works of art, found in the nineteenth century and transferred on this occasion from the Municipal Antiquarium on the Caelian hill, enriched the new museum section. At first, this structure was named the Mussolini Museum and later assumed the title, the Museo Nuovo. In this case, the arrangement of the works did not follow the new topographic systematization that Lanciani desired for the Museum of the Palazzo dei Conservatori. Instead, it followed a display criterion intended to reproduce the most significant milestones of Greek art through Roman copies inspired by Greek originals.

At the same time, in 1929, the exhibition spaces in the new Antiquarium on the Caelian hill were enlarged and completely renovated. The displays centered on the testimonies relative to the most ancient history of the city, from the origins to the Republican age. The Antiquarium also features objects of daily life in Rome dating to the imperial period.

After this period of renewal of the Capitoline museum structures, welcomed by the contemporary academic world with great enthusiasm, new serious problems arose concerning the collections placed under the jurisdiction of the Governorship. Two factors addressed the urgency of finding new spaces for the enlargement of the museum site. First, the premises of the Antiquarium on the Caelian hill after 1939 were unfit for use. Second, a noteworthy quantity of materials of great artistic and scientific relevance was found in various parts of the city (in particular, around the slopes of the Capitoline during the isolation of the hill).

Only in 1956, the creation of a new section of the Palazzo dei Conservatori, the Braccio Nuovo (New Wing) permitted the exposition of very important sculptures. The sculptures belonged to Republican and early imperial monuments found on the slopes of the Capitoline Hill and during the excavations conducted in Largo Argentina. During the same period, the underground gallery located beneath the Capitoline piazza was utilized as an exposition space for the Epigraphic Collection. The gallery constitutes an extraordinary axis linking the Palazzo dei Conservatori, Palazzo Nuovo, and Palazzo Senatorio (that contains the *Tabularium* and the Temple of Veiovis). The history of the Capitoline collections, which seems to have obtained its definitive form through post-war regulations, continued to develop. Indeed, the continuation of studies and research conducted within the museum and its numerous storerooms in these last decades led to important acquisitions of works of art and sculptural groups and the need for new presentations of previously studied material.

The restructuring of the Capitoline Museums that took place in distinct periods over a long span of time resulted in the recovery and creation of new spaces within the museum complex itself and the creation of a new decentralized museum site, the Montemartini Power Plant. During the restructuring of the Museo Nuovo, the discovery of the massive remains of the Temple of Capitoline Jupiter within the rooms rendered impossible the reorganization of these museum spaces according to the old arrangement. The Montemartini Power Plant, initially destined to provide a temporary display space for the Capitoline collections, instead, became the permanent site of a section of the collections because it is an ideal place to present sculptures to the public. The exceptionally large dimensions and luminosity of the spaces, and the striking contrast between the perfectly preserved machinery of the old electric power station and the brightness of the classical sculptures, constitute irremissible ingredients for the full utilization of an

The Capitoline Museums

The Formation of the Collections

extraordinary artistic patrimony. The architectural complex of the Temple of Apollo Sosianus, recently reassembled in its former monumental composition (due to the availability of suitable spaces), has a very important place in this patrimony. The new expansion of the Capitoline Museums and the new arrangement of the collections within the Palazzo dei Conservatori and the Clementino-Caffarelli complex are part of the completion of the enlargement of the exposition spaces included in the ambitious project "Great Capitoline Hill." They permit a suitable display of the equestrian statue of Marcus Aurelius, and they allow a better presentation of the sculptural complexes reorganized according to accurate historical and archival research.

PALAZZO NUOVO

PALAZZO
DEI CONSERVATORI
CLEMENTINO
CAFFARELLI

PALAZZO SENATORIO
TABULARIUM

MONTEMARTINI
POWER PLANT

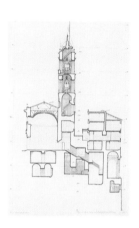

Ground Floor

 Ticket Office

 Capitoline Bookstore

 Checkroom

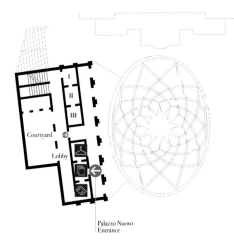

First Floor

   I Gallery
  II Hall of the Doves
 III Cabinet of Venus
 IV Hall of the Emperors
  V Hall of the Philosophers
 VI Great Hall
VII Hall of the Faun
VIII Hall of the Gladiator

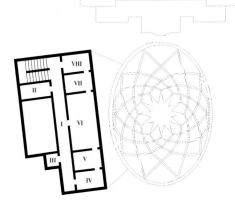

The palace located on the left of the piazza originally bore the name "Nuovo" (new) because it was constructed after the Palazzo Senatorio and the Palazzo dei Conservatori. Sixteenth century artwork depicts in its place a retaining wall of the convent of the Aracoeli that, today, overlooks the crowning of the internal courtyard. From the beginning, Michelangelo Buonarroti included the Palazzo Nuovo in the general design of his project. However, the palace was built after his death, and it was completed in several phases in the span of almost two centuries. The first stone was laid in 1603, under the auspices of Clement VIII. He entrusted the work to Girolamo Rainaldi, architect of the People of Rome. In 1614, only the foundations were complete. After a long pause, work began anew only in 1654, under the pontificate of Innocent X, who commissioned Carlo Rainaldi. He did his utmost to complete the construction of the building. From the beginning, the Palazzo Nuovo was destined to host famous masterpieces of Greek and Roman sculpture (already present in conspicuous numbers on the hill) in niches and aedicules, according to criteria "of the ancients." Drawings and written documents attest to the importance of Palazzo Nuovo. In fact, the building was the first to house an antiquarian patrimony of public property. For this reason, the palace was conceived as a division of external and internal spaces to optimally emphasize marbles located along the walls in gabled niches and intentionally open aedicules. The new building differs architecturally from the palaces of the Roman aristocracy that, already by the end of the sixteenth century, haphazardly preserved the memory of the ancients solely in outdoor contexts. Indeed, the Palazzo Nuovo constitutes a perfect, striking complex with a continuing alternation of wall divisions in plaster and travertine. Internally, Latin and Greek inscriptions and important reliefs decorate the walls.

The original "sky blue" color of the palace (recently restored), harmoniously synchronized with the terracotta pavement and wooden decorations of the wooden coffered ceilings and emphasized the marble material of the sculptures. The terracotta pavement was replaced in the nineteenth and twentieth centuries with large marble panels. Details of the ceiling, in part decorated with stucco and frescoes, were brought to light during the most recent work on the building. The architecture of the palace underwent noteworthy embellishments during the pontificate of Alexander VII (1655-1667)

and Clement X (1670-1676). Clement X commissioned the wooden ceilings
in the principal rooms. In the same years, the "Wool and Silk Guild," which
played a very important cultural role, obtained permission to use the building.
During this moment of concession, the inventory of the statues numbered 44.
In 1698, when the "Agricultural Arts" obtained permission to use the building,
the number of statues had increased to 50. In 1733, Pope Clement XII
inaugurated the new public collection of antiquity, organized according to the
criteria of a modern museum. The pope made a great effort to purchase the
sculptures that previously adorned the house of the Cardinal Alessandro Albani.
Cardinal Albani had meticulously formed a collection of ancient masterpieces that
originated in other collections and excavations. With the acquisition of the Albani
Collection, consisting of 418 sculptures, and the following acquisitions
and donations in 1745-1750, during the pontificate of Pope Benedict XIV,
the collections became very prestigious. As a result, the rooms were arranged
according to an itinerary, today substantially maintained, that also emphasized
the documentary value of the sculptures. In order to restore the statues, many
Roman sculptors were summoned. They reworked the surfaces, often mutilated,
to pristine condition. In many cases, their interpretation of the statues was very
learned. Between 1812 and 1818, the palace underwent many changes,
and the statues housed in the Church of Santa Maria in Aracoeli were acquired.
In 1816, in order to increase the existing space, the first room on the right
on the ground floor, called "The Inscription Hall" and the second small room,
called "Hall of the Urn", were resystematized. In 1990, the equestrian bronze
statue of Marcus Aurelius was transferred to the area occupied by the Egyptian
Collection (subsequently moved to the Palazzo dei Conservatori). The museum
contains works of ancient marble statues, displayed both according to an itinerary
that follows typological criteria (e.g., Hall of the Emperors, Hall of the
Philosophers) and also according to aesthetic principles that denote central
sculptures as "masterpieces" (e.g., Hall of the Faun, Hall of the Gladiator).
The collectors' predilection predominantly inspires the Gallery and the Great
Hall on the first floor, through the ornamental (rather than typological)
arrangement of the sculptures. This constitutes the first public collection
of antiquity that became the model for very important collections housed
in museums located throughout the world.

The internal space of the ground floor is articulated according to the architectural concept that seventeenth century palaces borrowed from the ancient Roman *domus*. The portico, divided by openings and niches symmetrically arranged and framed by architraves and columns in travertine, contains statues of large dimensions and some masterpieces once part of the Belvedere Collection in the Vatican and later donated to the City of Rome. The covered vaults (part barrel and part arched) create a particular variation of light and offer a visual effect that culminates in the central part that leads to the internal courtyard. Above, large shell-shaped ornaments scenographically complete the decoration. Roman inscriptions, for the most part funerary, are inserted in the walls.

Statue of Minerva

The sculpture, of colossal dimensions (over three meters high) previously was located on the piazza at the base of the staircase of the Palazzo Senatorio and in the portico of the Palazzo dei Conservatori.

The goddess is represented standing, with her weight resting on her right leg, and her left leg slightly bent. She wears a large chiton, with folds rendered with a flat chisel. Around her waist, a large belt holds the chiton in place. Holes, to which attachments in metal were added, are visible on the belt. Some holes for the attachment of parts consisting of different material are visible on the *apoptygma*, on the chest. The head and the arms are assembled according to the conception of large acroliths. The head, covered by a helmet, has hollow eye cavities originally filled with hard stones and metal. Therefore, the sculpture is a direct inspiration from the famous chryselephantine (in gold and ivory) statue that Pheidias created for the Athenian temple of the goddess in the middle of the fifth century BC. Possibly, the statue was created by Greek craftsmanship in the second century BC for a very important temple.

Statue of the empress Faustina the Elder
The empress, the wife of Antoninus Pius
(AD 138-161), appears in the guise
of the goddess Ceres, protectress
of agriculture. Her left hand tightly holds
a cornucopia. Recent restoration
of the statue has revealed the remains
of gilding on her face and among the locks
of hair, and the remains of metal
on her chest, perhaps decorated with
a metal pectoral.

Female statue with portrait-head
The sculpture had been located in the
Belvedere Vatican collection and it was
inserted, together with a portrait-head
statue of Livia and another very similar
portrait, known as Aspasia,
on a moulding located above the Marforio
until 1818. Today, all of the statues
are housed within the lobby.
The figure is standing. A long chiton,
a heavy mantle (draped over her left arm),
and a band cover her body.

The portrait-head, not related to the statue,
is ancient and datable to the late second
century AD.
The body is a Roman copy of the Aphrodite
Sosandra that Kalamis created in the fifth
century BC. Roman replicas were
very common in the second century AD,
and many reproductions were utilized
as iconic statues of noble Roman women.

Fountain in the Courtyard
with the "Marforio" statue

The middle of the lobby connects to the courtyard. The statue called "Marforio"
overlooks a fountain that is part of the scenographic wall enclosing the far end
of the courtyard. The statue is called Marforio because in the sixteenth century
it was believed that the statue was found in the Forum of Mars (*Martis Forum*,
the name that the ancients gave to the Forum of Augustus). In 1594, Bescapè
added the typical attributes of Ocean to the colossal-scale statue. Many scholars
identify it as a representation of the Tiber or some other river divinity
that adorned a fountain in antiquity.

Long hair, a beard, and a very thick moustache characterize the tilted head
of the figure reclining on his left side. Stylistically the piece dates to the Flavian
period (first century AD). During the Renaissance it enjoyed particular notoriety
because Romans affixed "pasquinate" to it. "Pasquinate" are defamatory writings
against the government that the people signed with the name Pasquino.

Statues of Satyrs

The two statues placed on either side
of the fountain in niches and known
as the Satyrs of the Valley were found
in Rome near the Theater of Pompey.
They were preserved for a long period
of time not far from where they were
discovered, i.e., in the courtyard of the
Palazzo della Valle. These two mirroring
statues that depict Pan, the Greek god
of the countryside and nature, are linked
to the cult of Dionysus. This divinity,
half-man and half-goat with a bearded face
and ferine horns, also is defined
unequivocally by the panther skin draped
over the chest. Each Capitoline image
preserves a statue in high relief depicting
a figure with an upraised arm that sticks
out, holding a basket full of bunches
of grapes balanced on its head.
They have been considered decorations
of the Theater of Pompey and utilized
as Telamones, statues used as architectural
structures of support. The fine modeling
of the surfaces and the excellent
workmanship suggest that they are works
of the late Hellenistic period, and possibly
were placed either in a small portico
or a loggia connected to the area
of the theater.

Equestrian statue of the emperor
Marcus Aurelius (AD 161-180)
Recent restoration has returned
this famous bronze statue to its former
extraordinary beauty. The statue once
belonged to a triumphal monument.
It depicts the emperor Marcus Aurelius
in his mature years, majestic and charismatic
and in a pose characterized by a peaceful
gesture that summarizes his martial
vicissitudes. In fact, he spent a great part
of his rule defending the borders of the
empire, besieged by the barbarian
populations of Germany.
The equestrian group, perhaps already
gilded in antiquity, was spared from
being melted down and was placed
in the piazza because it is was believed
to represent Constantine "in the act
of blessing," symbol of Christianity.
Like all colossal bronze statues, the Marcus
Aurelius statue was constructed
out of separate pieces soldered together.
A faithful copy of the statue stands
in the piazza in place of the original
that was transferred into the courtyard
of the museum.

Group of Polyphemus

The group represents Polyphemus who grips a young boy lying at his feet.

The work, missing the right arm of the Cyclops and the head of the small boy, comes from the Vatican Collections.

In 1636, the Conservators inscribed on the base the date of the piece's acquisition. At this time, both the arm with the *syrinx* and the head were added according to the hypothesis that the two figures were "Pan and a small boy." Polyphemus is nude, seated on a rock with a ferine skin draped on his thigh. A third eye characterizes his face, a distinctive feature of the Cyclops, the son of the god of the sea, Poseidon. The group illustrates one of the most salient moments from the *Odyssey*, when Ulysses and his companions find themselves in the cave of Polyphemus. This group (dating to the late imperial period), possibly pertains to the Hellenistic archetype of Ulysses, who extends the cup to Polyphemus.

Colossal statue of Mars

The colossal statue was found in two parts, torso and detached head, in the sixteenth century nearby the Forum of Nerva. Until the end of the eighteenth century, the statue was identified as Pyrrhus, the famous king of Epirus. It is an image of Mars, represented standing, wearing a *lorica* (military breastplate that recalls the martial activity and ensuing peace of which the god was the guarantor). The decoration of the breastplate is very rich; it depicts the head of Medusa and two winged griffins flanking a candelabrum upheld by a palmette.

Among many other decorations, the masks and pairs of elephant heads led to the identification of the statue as Pyrrhus. There are many noteworthy modern additions, including the shield, part of the helmet, and legs that appear squat and shortened (although they are adorned with impressive boots). The head of the god, with a rich beard, curly hair, and Corinthian helmet, suggests that the sculpture dates to the Flavian age (first century AD). Probably the statue was located outside the Temple of Mars Ultor in substitution of the original cult statue, damaged by a serious fire.

The "Small ground floor rooms" identify the three spaces on the ground floor
to the right of the lobby.
At the conclusion of the construction of the Palazzo Nuovo, every single space
was accessible to the portico. Only in the eighteenth-nineteenth centuries
and following periods even these rooms were designated as exhibition spaces.
In particular, the ground floor rooms on the right house very important
epigraphic monuments. Among these number the fragments of the post-Caesarian
Roman calendars, all of which record the new year that Caesar defined
as 365 days, and the magistrate list called "the Minor *Fasti*," in relation
to the more famous *Fasti* exhibited in the Palazzo dei Conservatori.
The first room houses many portraits of private Romans, among which one
of the most important is that related to a member of the Julio-Claudian family,
maybe Germanicus, son of Drusus the Elder, or Drusus the Elder himself
(middle of the first century AD).

Funerary relief

The funerary relief, of unknown origin, depicts three male figures inside a niche with a flat border. The man in the center seems the oldest, the one for whom the relief was commissioned. In fact, the writing "*VIV(VS)*" placed under the other two clarifies that they were still alive at the time of the creation of the piece. The three men are represented according to the dress and pose proper of funerary reliefs: half busts, in frontal poses, dressed in tunic and toga, out of which appears the right hand.

In the late Republican and Augustan periods, this type of relief was used especially by the middle class of freedmen, i.e., freed slaves. Therefore, it is possible also in this case that the three people were linked not by the bonds of kinship but of slavery. They could have been part of a unique *familia*.

Funerary urn of Titus Statilius Aper
The altar-funerary urn, found on the Janiculum, was transported through the orders of Paul III to the Belvedere in the Vatican (1542). In 1743, Benedict XIV ordered its transfer to the Capitoline Museum.
The sepulchral monument, noteworthy for its dimensions and decoration, was sculpted on three sides. There is an unfinished cavity in the back, which must have contained vases for the ashes.

Two inscriptions are engraved on the plinth. One records that two parents dedicate the altar to their son, *Titus Statilius Aper, mensor aedificiorum* – a sort of master builder – and to their daughter-in-law *Orcivia Anthis*. The other inscription is a metrical play on the last name *Aper*, which in Latin means boar, through reference to the mythical boar hunted by Meleager. The instruments, which *Statilius* used in work, appear on both sides of the funerary urn. The portrait

of his wife is located in a seashell at the center of the crowning. Stylistically and epigraphically, the tomb dates to the first century AD, when the dead predominantly were cremated.

Attic sarcophagus with scenes depicting the life of Achilles

In 1582, or a little before, a private citizen found this imposing sarcophagus outside Porta San Giovanni, between the Via Latina and Via Labicana, in a mausoleum known as "Mount of Grain."
The sarcophagus, a *kline* (bed) type produced in Attica, is one of the largest of this kind ever found. All four sides are decorated. In the back, the decoration is in unfinished low relief, maybe because it was placed against a wall in the tomb.
The deceased couple is represented in a reclining pose on the lid.
The physiognomy of the faces dates the work to the second century AD.
The sculptural narration centers on the figure of Achilles. On the frontal side, the youth brandishes a sword, freeing himself from his female dress. Ulysses discovered the Greek hero, hidden on Scyros among the daughters of Lycomedes, in order to avoid the Trojan War.

On the sides of the scene sit king Agamemnon, on the right, and Lycomedes, on the left. The left side represents Achilles, who departs from Lycomedes. On the back, he prepares for his duel against Hector. On the right side, finally, Priam asks for the restitution of his deceased son's body.

The wide staircase joins the ground floor to the first floor of the museum.
Reliefs belonging to sarcophagi of the late imperial period are inserted
on the back walls. Within the aedicules are sculptures. The head of the statue
on the right is unrelated to the body, probably an original of the Hellenistic age.
After the second ramp, one arrives in the Gallery of the museum.
The long Gallery, which extends the entire length of the Capitoline Museum,
connects different exhibition rooms. It offers to the visitor a variety of statue
collections, portraits, reliefs, and inscriptions displayed by the eighteenth century
Conservators in a casual manner. Indeed, they were more concerned
with producing architectural symmetry and a general ornamental effect
than accurate historical, artistic, and archaeological documentation.
The overall effect is disorganized and inhomogeneous, but it preserves an
exceptional example of the historical past. Inscriptions of small dimensions are
inserted and framed on the walls. Among them is a consistent group originating
from a common tomb (*columbarium*) of the freedmen and freedwomen of Livia.
The sculptures are illustrated beginning with the left wall.

Colossal statue of Hercules
The sculpture was discovered during
the reconstruction of the Church
of Sant'Agnese fuori le Mura. The sculptor
Alessandro Algardi (1602-1654)
conducted a complete restoration of the
statue. He probably modified the ancient
iconography of Hercules who domesticates
the hind of Ceryneia to the iconography
of Hercules who kills the Hydra.
At any rate, the work is a Roman reworking
(dating to the second century AD)
of a Greek creation attributed to Lysippus.

Statue of a wounded warrior
The torso constitutes the only ancient
part of this prestigious and famous statue.
It seems to be an optimal reworking of the
Discobolos that Myron made in 460 BC.
The interpretation of the statue as a
wounded warrior in the moment of falling
is the product of the reworking
of the sculpture by Pierre Etienne Monnot,
who lived from 1658 to 1733.

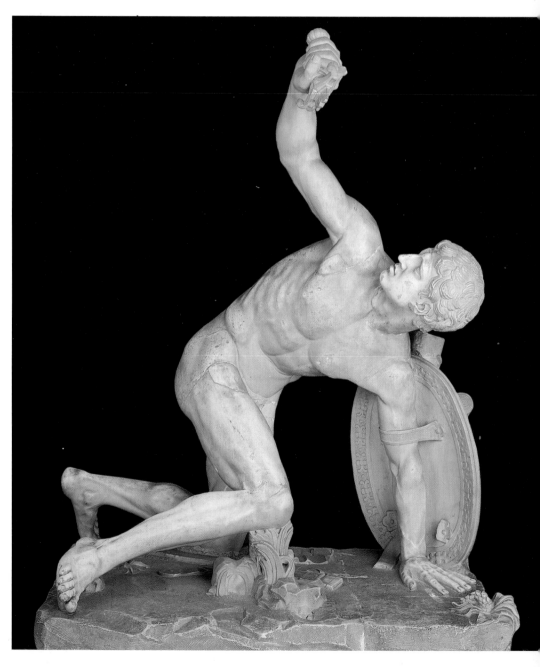

Eros who strings his bow
This is one of the best imperial age copies,
derived from Lysippus' famous creation.
It represents the youthful, winged god
in the act of stringing the bow that he used
to shoot his arrows of love.

MUNIFICENTIA·SS·D·N·BENEDICTI
PP·XIV·A·D·MDCCLIII

*Statuette of baby Hercules who strangles
the snakes*
The statuette represents a real baby,
depicted as the little hero. It has been
interpreted as a portrait of baby Caracalla,
or, more recently, Annius Verus,
the emperor Marcus Aurelius' son.

Statue of Leda and the swan
This group is a sculptural representation of the erotic theme of Leda and Zeus in the guise of a swan. Leda, partially nude, is depicted in the act of lifting up her mantle with her left arm in order to protect the swan from the eagle in the act of snatching it. With her right hand, she holds the swan. The figure is leaning on a tree trunk placed to her right. The statue could be a reworking of a group attributed to the Greek Timotheos, in the fourth century BC, and very common in many replicas beginning in the first century BC.

The room on the right derives its name from the pavement mosaic found in 1737 in Hadrian's Villa in Tivoli. It is preserved, for the most part, in its eighteenth century phase. At that time, the room was called "Hall of the Miscellaneous Objects" because it contained works of typologically diverse material.
All of the pieces belonged to the collection of Cardinal Alessandro Albani, the first acquisition of the Capitoline Museum.
Male and female portraits of private citizens, arranged at the time on shelves along the walls, currently are ordered in the same way, with the exception of some alterations. In 1817, the large marble crater with vegetal decorations located in the center of the room changed the name of the space to the "Hall of the Vase". Today the vase is located along the back wall of the Gallery of the Capitoline Museum.
During the first half of the eighteenth century, numerous Roman sepulchral inscriptions were used to decorate the upper part of the walls of this room. The arrangement of the inscriptions has never been altered.
The finds visible in the glass display cases are recorded in the list of acquisitions of the eighteenth century. Most noteworthy among the pieces displayed are the following: bronze *tabula* (third century AD) recording the honorific title of patron that the guild of the *Fabri* of *Sentinum* (Sassoferrato, in the Marche Region) bestowed to *Coretius Fuscus*; the *Tabula Iliaca*, a fragment of a miniature plaque in low relief (first century BC) with scenes from Homer's *Iliad* accompanied by explicit inscriptions; a bronze inscription from the Aventine, recording a dedication of the Fourth Cohort of the *Vigiles* to Septimius Severus and the imperial family in AD 203; the Decree of Pompeius Strabo, which conceded particular privileges to some Spanish knights who fought on the side of the Romans at the battle of Asculum, during the Social War (90-89 BC); the Senatusconsultum regarding Asclepiades of Klazomenes and his allies, the oldest remains of a Senate decree in bronze (78 BC), almost entirely preserved. One reads on the decree the conferral of the title *amici populi Romani* to three Greek navarchs that had fought on the side of the Romans during the Social War, or, perhaps, the Sullan War (83-82 BC). The text is in Latin, with a Greek translation appearing on the lower part of the tablet. The Greek text permitted a reconstruction of the fragmentary Latin text.

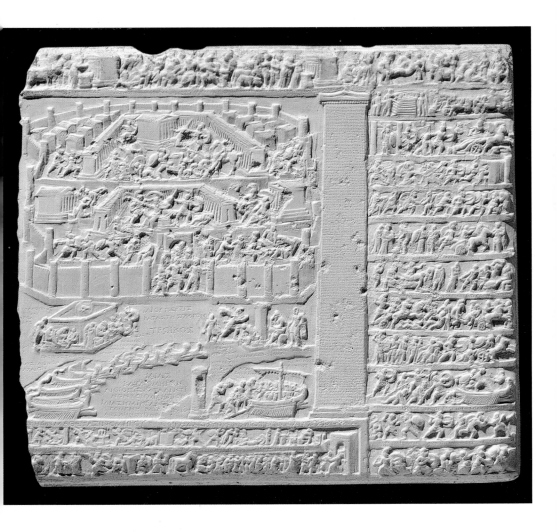

Mosaic of the Doves

The mosaic, which gives the room its name, was found in 1737, at the center of a pavement, in a room in Hadrian's Villa at Tivoli. The scene is composed of four doves, one of which drinks, balanced on the rim of a bronze bowl. A figure in relief seems to uphold the handle. An astragal pattern recalling architectural motifs decorates the frame.

Nevertheless, the mosaic is not entirely preserved. The border decorated with a garland, which was part of the Albani Collection, was donated to Frederick of Saxony.

Now, it is on display in the Augusteum in Dresda. The mosaic is a figured panel (*émblema*) composed of very tiny polychromatic marble and glass *tesserae*, placed at the center of a Hadrianic-period room. This type of decoration, produced in the Roman period for rich clients, is distinct from the other kinds of mosaic pavement, thereby constituting its high worth. The *émblema* is a copy of the work of Sosos, active in Pergamon in the second century BC. We have other copies of this work, including the mosaic in the House of the Faun in Pompeii, that differ in particular details. The mosaic from Hadrian's Villa (second century AD) is the closest to the original scheme. The high level of skill employed in its production creates a surprising pictorial effect.

Mosaic of theatrical masks

In 1824, the mosaic was found in the vineyards of the Jesuits on the Aventine, in front of the Church of Santa Prisca, on the site of the baths constructed by Trajan Decius (AD 249-251). Pope Leo XII (1823-1829) acquired them and placed them in this room. The mosaic represents two masks leaning on a socle projecting out from two walls that meet at an angle, seen in perspective. Two flutes lean on one wall. Their shadows project onto the wall.

The female mask depicts a woman with large eyes and wide-open mouth. A ribbon, knotted into a bow at the center of her brow, appears in her curly hair with long ringlets. The physiognomic features of the man are exaggerated and ridiculed. The mouth is enormous. The nose is large and squashed. The eyes bulge out, and the cheeks are wrinkled. On his head is a crown of ivy and berries, decoration associated with the cult of Dionysus, which was linked closely to the birth of the Greek theater. The masks belong to two "types" from New Comedy, which developed in the Hellenistic period: the young woman, often sad for her misfortunes and the slave, fearful and mocking. The work, constructed with polychromatic marble *tesserae* by an artist attentive of perspective and the effect of light and shade, probably belonged to an *émblema* pavement in an imperial building on the Aventine. It is thought to date to the second century AD, maybe the Hadrianic period.

Statue of a young girl with dove
The statue, located at the center
of the room, depicts a girl who protects
a dove from the attack of a snake by hiding
the dove in the folds of the mantle covering
her long tunic. The snake is the product
of modern restoration.
The statue is a Roman copy of a Hellenistic
original. In the Hellenistic age attention
to the aspects of daily life, in all its forms,
developed. Typical of this genre is the
representation of children, often depicted
at play, as in this sculpture. In particular,
the figurative motif of the young girl with
the dove finds a possible antecedent
in the reliefs of the Greek funerary stelai
of the fifth and fourth centuries BC.

Funerary urn of Lucilius Felix
According to the testimony of Pirro
Ligorio, the urn was found in a tomb,
on the Via Appia, and the lid probably does
not pertain to the urn.
In every facet of the octagonal-shaped
urn is the representation of a little Cupid.
Three play musical instruments, one
carries a lantern, another lights his torch,
and the last one dances. Above each Cupid
is a decoration of laurel, vines, and satyr
masks. The work is a delicate construction,
probably dating to the Neronian age.

Statue of a drunken old woman
The sculpture, reassembled from many
fragments and heavily restored, depicts an
old woman tightly holding onto a wine vase.
The work appears on the list of Hellenistic
representations of personages devoted
to vices and represented in their degraded
level of daily life. The rendering of the veins
and wrinkling of the skin is very realistic,
with particular attention to the drapery,
suggesting that this is a copy of a work
executed in the third century BC at Smyrna
by a Myron known for his *anus ebria*.

Colossal heads of goddesses
Two heads of large dimensions are placed
one in front of the other.
They are the remaining fragments of cult
statues that were sculpted in separate
pieces, according to the acrolithic
technique. This type of sculpture possibly
was made in Rome by sculptors
of Attic origin, active in the second century
BC (according to literary sources).

The small polygonal room located at three-quarter's length of the Gallery was created in the first decades of the nineteenth century. It provides a striking setting, typical of a fountain, for the famous Capitoline Venus statue.

Capitoline Venus

The sculpture, of slightly larger than life size dimensions, was found near the Basilica of San Vitale around 1667-1670. In 1752, Pope Benedict XIV acquired it and donated it to the Capitoline collections. It is one of the most famous statues of the museum and boasts a series of reproductions that are located in many other international collections. It is made of precious marble (probably Parian), and represents Venus-Aphrodite nude and in contemplation, coming out of her bath. She is depicted with her arms following the curving contours of her soft and fleshy small-boned body and covering her breasts and pubic area. The right leg is forward and bent, and the left is resting. The head is slightly tilted towards the left. The hairstyle is complicated. Part of the hair is pulled up, in the form of hoops, at the top of her head and tied to form a bow. Other locks touch her shoulders. The expression of the face seems absent, psychologically depicted by the small, languid eyes and the small, fleshy mouth.

This sculpture defines the so-called "Capitoline type," of which today one hundred replicas are known. It may be a variation of the Pudica Venus type. Scholars have debated at length regarding the chronology of the image of the goddess and the chronology of the copies. The Capitoline Venus could be one of the first and most faithful replicas. Like all of the other depictions of this type, it was destined to decorate an ancient complex of noteworthy sophistication, in the first century BC.

From the opening of the museum to the public in 1734, the curators of the artistic collections displayed in this room in the Capitoline Museum all of the busts, herms, and portraits depicting Roman emperors, and personages of the imperial circle, both securely identified and purely deduced. The works on display are the product of a reasoned selection from the collection during the nineteenth century, eventually reduced and rearranged according to more rigorous and consequential historical and logical-thematic criteria. Today in the Hall of the Emperors, 67 busts and portraits are on display, and in the center is a seated statue of a woman. Eight ancient reliefs and a modern, honorary inscription adorn the walls.

The busts, arranged for the most part in a double row on marble shelves, allow the visitor to follow chronologically the development of Roman portraiture from the Republican period to the late-antique period by offering quantitatively and, more importantly, qualitatively rich illustrations.

The itinerary winds along in a helicoidal fashion in a clockwise direction. Entering from the Hall of the Philosophers, the itinerary starts from the upper shelf immediately to the left, and it terminates at the end of the lower shelf, immediately to the right of the same entrance. The collection includes two portraits of Augustus. The first is related to the moment immediately following his victorious battle of Actium (31 BC), which marked his ascent to the throne. The second depicts the emperor already in full maturity, his head crowned by a triumph wreath of oak leaves. He seems serene and wise and aware of his *auctoritas*. This portrait of Augustus is similar to the portrait of the empress Livia, his wife, embellished with a rich and tall diadem decorated with ears of wheat and flower buds. She appears in the guise of the benevolent fertile goddess Ceres.

Likewise, in the series of portraits relating to the earliest part of the imperial age, one of the most noteworthy portraits is that of Agrippina the Elder, unlucky wife of Germanicus, depicted with a typical rendering of the hair consisting of small curls on her brow. Another important portrait is the very rare depiction of Nero, very young and related to the early part of his reign.

In the series of emperors from the Flavian dynasty are the important portraits of Vespasian, Titus, Julia, and Nerva.

The collection of portraits dating to the second century AD is particularly

Portrait of "Actian type"
Augustus

Portrait of Agrippina the Elder

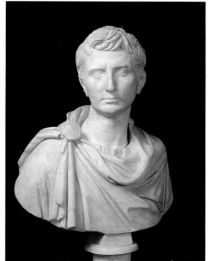

complete and exhaustive. Among the portraits the most outstanding are Trajan and Plotina, Hadrian, Antoninus Pius and Faustina the Elder, Marcus Aurelius and Faustina the Younger, Lucius Verus, and Commodus. In the male series of the emperors, one can follow the evolution of the hair and beard style. In the beginning the faces were clean-shaven, and later, the beard was worn long, "in Greek fashion," with the intent of appearing inspired and philosophically committed. In the female series, one can follow the development of hairstyles, from the tall, stacked, "scaffolded" hairstyles typical of the Flavian tradition, to those characterized by a ring-shaped bun (of varying size), typical of the entire Antonine period.

The Severan household (AD 193-217) is also well represented. It includes the portraits of the following: Septimius Severus, placed on an imposing bust of green alabaster, Julia Domna, his wife, and his children Geta and Caracalla. In addition, there are portraits of Elagabalus, Maximinus of Thrace, Trajan Decius, Aurelius Probus, and Diocletian.

The imperial series ends with the head of the young Honorius (AD 384–423), the youngest child of the emperor Theodosius, in prelude to the figurative modes of Byzantine art.

The room contains numerous female portraits, with complicated hairstyles and, in some cases, wigs with very elaborate curls. Among these the most outstanding are the portrait of Faustina the Elder (wife of Antoninus Pius) and Faustina the Younger, who changed her hairstyle every time she gave birth to a child. Eight different hairstyles of Faustina the Younger are known. The portrait of "the Flavian woman," who has a complex and articulated hairstyle and sophisticated facial features, is very prestigious. The polychromatic bust of a Roman woman, whose portrait comes from Smyrna and dates to the period of Alexander Severus, is unique. It was constructed out of distinct pieces, with the separate insertion of hair, like many other busts of this type belonging to this period. The hair, maybe lost, was restored in modern times with *nero antico* marble.

Beginning with the foundation of the Capitoline Museum, this room, located next
to the Hall of the Emperors, was created to house and display the portraits, busts,
and herms depicting poets, philosophers, and orators from ancient Greece
of the Classical and Hellenistic periods. In the Roman age, these portraits
(according to the vogue introduced by the erudite Asinius Pollio in the second
half of the first century BC) decorated public and private libraries, houses of the
nobles, villas and parks of wealthy, sensitive connoisseurs of arts and philosophy.
Renaissance collectors embellished their palaces and their collections with
the most representative images of many illustrious men.

Currently the Hall of the Philosophers displays 79 portraits. The identity of many
portraits has been ascertained. Many portraits certainly are "reconstructions,"
i.e., created long after the death of the individual, and therefore only vaguely
resemble the real physiognomic features. Others, instead, beginning in the
Hellenistic period, reproduce, with great accuracy, the different physiognomies.
The collection begins with a numerous representation of herms depicting Homer,
the most famous poet in antiquity. He is depicted conventionally as an old man,
with a thick beard and hair. His eyes are already lifeless, corresponding not only
to his legendary blindness but also the profound sensitivity and awareness
of the soul and the destiny of man. The prototype of this portrait can be attributed
to an artistic Rhodian school and can be dated close to 200 BC.

The portrait of Pindar, another famous Greek poet, is a reconstruction.
Its statuary prototype dates back to an artistic moment influenced by the Severe
style (first half of the fifth century BC).

The portrait identified as Pythagoras, the famous philosopher and mathematician
of Samos, is interesting. A flat turban wrapped around his head characterizes
this portrait.

Socrates is depicted according to the portrait created by Lysippus around
the middle of the fourth century BC, about half a century after the death of the
philosopher. He is almost depicted as a satyr, with an upward turned, fleshy nose,
round and protruding eyes, rounded brow, and wide mouth with swollen lips.

In addition, there are portraits depicting the three most famous Athenian tragic
poets. The features of the face of Aeschylus are full and defined, decorated
by a stylized and ornamental beard, maybe deriving from a prototype of about
the middle of the fifth century BC. Sophocles has a squared and solid head.

Herm of Euripides   Bust of Cicero

His beard and hair have short, rich locks, tied by a ribbon. Euripides is depicted as a man in his mature years, with a receding hairline and long hair that covers his ears. The prototype, which can be dated to 320 BC, preserves the traces of Lysippan style.

Among the many portraits of famous individuals from the Greek world, many original portraits from the Roman period are displayed in this room.

The bust of Cicero, famous statesman and man of letters, is depicted in his early 50s, at the peak of his intellectual and political powers. The general conception of this portrait is based on Greek portraiture during the late Hellenistic era. However, realistic features that belong to the more authentic Roman portraiture of the Republican age are clearly evident.

Because of its ample, monumental size, this room constitutes the most
representative space of the entire Capitoline museum complex.
The "Large hall in the middle" was decorated and designed to create harmony
between the exhibition space and the displayed statues. The four walls are divided
into vertical sections. In these sections, the cadence of the architectural order
evenly distributes the studied division of the room. The large seventeenth century
coffers on the ceiling harmonize with the walls. The diversity of the geometric
forms of the coffers, composed of octagonal, rectangular, and other shapes,
expresses the magnificence typical of the Baroque style. The engraving
on the rosettes, variously carved, enhances the richness of the ceiling. The crest
of Pope Innocent X Pamphili, who was responsible for the completion of the
palace, is located in the center of the ceiling. Recent restoration has recuperated
the colors of the surfaces by emphasizing the richness of the composition.
A large door located on the long wall adjoining the Gallery is especially
interesting. In the first half of the eighteenth century, Filippo Barigioni designed
the portal as an arch with two winged Victories of very high quality.

Apollo with the lyre

In 1734, Clement XII purchased the statue for the sum of 1000 *scudi* from the Duke of Palombara. The statue is a Roman copy of a reworking of the Apollo Lykeios, depicted with a lyre, by Praxiteles. Two sources testify that the original statue was located in Athens. First, the statue is depicted on some coins, and second, a brief note by the poet Lucian, who does not mention the author of the work, depicts the deity with a bow, at rest after a long exertion. This statue type was the object of many reworkings, until the late Hellenistic period. Therefore, the attribute of the statue to Praxiteles is uncertain. The Apollo with the lyre from the Capitoline Museum is one of the most complete reworkings closest to the original type. The lyre resting on the tripod acting as a support substitutes the bow. The god does not seem tired, resting after a heavy exertion. Rather, he seems concentrated in a moment of inspiration. This work bears the stamp of an original because here the psychological element that appears is in contrast to the other reposing statue, which conveys the feelings of tiredness. It is not possible to attribute the statue of Apollo playing the lyre to Praxiteles or to his children. It is probably a later variant created in the Hellenistic age, ascribable to the Attic sculptor, Timarchides, who lived in the first half of the second century BC. At this time he was commissioned to create a statue of Apollo for the Circus Flaminius. He is the progenitor of a family of sculptors active in Rome during the entire second century BC, according to Pliny the Elder (*Natural History*, XXXVI, 35).

Apollo of the Omphalos
The Apollo of the *Omphalos* is thus named because one of the best preserved copies in the Museum of Athens depicts the *omphalós*. The *omphalós* is a rock covered by a net that was venerated in Delphi. The Capitoline statue, originating from the Albani Collection, is a well made Roman copy of the Greek original attributed to Kalamis (470-460 BC). Some scholars identify it as the Apollo *Alexíkakos*, who wards off evil, vowed at Athens for the healing after the pestilence of 430-427 BC. Others identify it as the prototype of the Apollo sculpted by Onathas (490-460 BC).

Three elements of the statue indicate that it was created in the period of time between the end of the Severe style and beginning of the Classical style. They are the anatomical structure, rendered with the essential masses, the face of god, which has a benevolent expression, and the hairstyle "tightly braided" around the head.

The hunter with the hare
In 1747, the statue was found near Porta Latina. It depicts a nude youth that shows his prey, a hare. He leans on the spear held in his left hand. Altogether, this work represents a *pastiche* of the third century AD. The portrait depicts a personage of the second century AD, according to its similarity to works dating to the rule of Gallienus. Instead, the body depends on a Greek original dating to the middle of the fifth century BC, representing Perseus in the act of lifting up the head of Medusa.

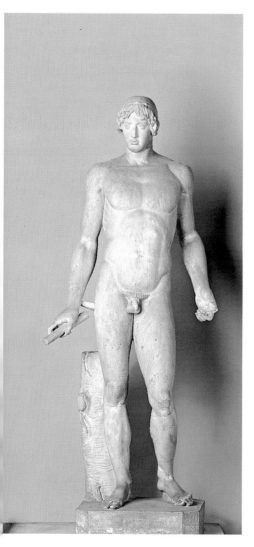

Harpocrates

In 1741, the statue was found in a room in the substructures of the "Pecile" in Hadrian's Villa. In 1744 Benedict XIV donated it to the Capitoline collections. The god, son of Isis and Osiris, is represented nude, without pubic hair. The body type is soft and fleshy. He leans his weight on his right leg. Behind it, up to the height of the knee, is the representation of a palm trunk covered in fruit.

The left leg is slightly bent and placed slightly back. The pelvic line is just visible, and the stomach is round and slightly prominent. The buttocks, round and well defined, underline the young age of the god. The right arm, just moved ahead, is bent. The hand rests at the height of his right nipple, and his index finger is raised and attached to his chin by a small strut. The arm is placed so that the finger brushes the lower lip, in the habitual gesture of silence. In the Roman period

this gesture was interpreted as mystic, intended to insure the secrets of the religion. The left arm, held away from the body by a strut located at the height of the hips, extends ahead and bends. The left hand tightly holds a horn in its well-modeled fingers. The head, of refined workmanship, tilts to the left, in order to underline the particular expression of the child. The locks of hair, rendered with delicate carving, rest above the brow, to form short bangs. The hair is

pulled up and held in place with a ribbon. This tuft of gathered hair supports a smooth hat, called the *pschent* (the motif representing the crown of Lower and Middle Egypt). Competent use of the drill in the hair and irises, depicted through the depression in the eyeball, suggests that the sculpture dates to the Hadrianic period. Perhaps the iconography of the figure is similar to an Alexandrine original, derived from a Praxitelean work, also known through numerous miniature bronze statuettes.

"Capitoline type" Amazon
This statue is also known as the "Sosikles' type" because of the signature present on this important replica. The statue belonged to the Albani Collection. It is larger than life size and generally is attributed to the work of Polyclitus. Napolioni, instructor of Cavaceppi, restored the work. The right arm is raised, possibly originally holding a spear, on which the figure leaned. The head is turned toward the right leg, whereas the left arm holds up the hem of the drapery to reveal her wound.

"Furietti" Centaurs

Located in the center of the room, the two statues were found in Hadrian's Villa in Tivoli during Cardinal Furietti's excavation. In 1765, Clement XIII acquired the statues for the Capitoline Museum. Aristeas and Papias, artists from Aphrodisias, a city in Asia Minor, signed the sculptures, made of *bigio morato* marble. Aphrodisias had a school of skillful copyists of Greek works. In the last decades of the first century AD, some of these artists moved to Rome, where the munificence of the emperors and private citizens provided continual, well-rewarded work.

The majority of the most known sculptures, including the Centaurs of the Capitoline, date to the rule of Hadrian (second century AD).

These statues are very famous due to the great skill and the rarity of the material, a prized marble extracted from the quarries on the promontory of Cape Tenaros in Lakonia. Anatomic details and distinction in the depiction of the features of the faces help characterize the age and emotions of the Centaurs.

The young Centaur is happy and joyful. The old Centaur is old and suffering. The attempt to render the hair, beard, and tails with a metallic effect is evident and suggests that the statues derive from original ones constructed in bronze.

The hall acquired this name in 1817, when the statue of the Faun was placed in the center of the room. Inscriptions inserted in the eighteenth century cover the walls, divided into groups according to their content. One section is devoted to brickstamps. On the right wall, the *Lex de imperio Vespasiani* (first century AD) stands out among the epigraphic texts. This decree confers special power to the emperor Vespasian. This precious document, recorded from the fourteenth century on the Capitoline Hill, is constructed of bronze with a particular technique. The text is not engraved but written when the metal was still hot.

Drunken faun in rosso antico *marble*
The sculpture, in precious *rosso antico* marble, was discovered in 1736. Clemente Bianchi and Bartolomeo Cavaceppi were entrusted with the delicate and arduous restoration. They added many pieces of *rosso granato* marble, characterized by obvious grayish veins. They did not particularly modify the structure or the ancient image. As early as 1746, when it was purchased for the Capitoline collections, the sculpture aroused the admiration of travelers

and cataloguers of the museum.
The figure leans on his right leg. The left leg, which conforms to the original, is slightly forward and shows the foot rotated outward, indicating the rhythm of the dance. The pelvic line is delineated clearly. Engraved furrows slightly mark the partition of the abdominal muscles. The lower margin of the abdomen is semicircular. The upper part of the torso, decorated by a *nebrís* (faun skin) knotted on the right shoulder, is characterized by masses of muscle well

defined and by the impression of the ribs. The face, framed by long sideburns divided into locks, has protruding cheekbones. The half-opened mouth forms a smile, revealing a row of teeth. The empty eye sockets probably were filled with metals or hard stones. Perhaps, this type was utilized in the decorative context of *horti*, exactly coinciding with the exaltation of bucolic motifs. It was a common statue type in the Roman period that reproduced themes from the late Hellenistic period, i.e., the late second century BC.

This room takes its name from the central sculpture (the Capitoline Gaul).
Alessandro Capponi, president of the Capitoline Museum, purchased the statue.
At the time of its acquisition, the statue was identified erroneously as a gladiator
in the act of falling on his shield.

Amazon

Generally, the sculpture is identified as the wounded Amazon type based on Pheidias' statue of the same subject. It is thought that Pheidias reutilized the theme of the conquered Amazon, dear to the Athenian culture of the fifth century BC. The delicate and luminescent rendering of the drapery is similar to the Amazons depicted on the frieze of the Parthenon. The support is on the right leg, and the right arm is raised to hold a bow.

The statue comes from Villa d'Este (located inside the ancient perimeter of Hadrian's Villa). In 1753 Pope Benedict XIV donated it to the Capitoline collections. Interpretation of the type is difficult because of consistent restorations. Indeed, Bartolomeo Cavaceppi (responsible for a great number of eighteenth century interpolations) almost completely replicated the motif of the wounded Amazon.

Resting Satyr

In 1753 Pope Benedict XIV donated the statue to the Capitoline Museum. After the Treaty of Tolentino, it was handed over to the French. It was returned to the Capitoline collections in 1815. The sculpture represents a young Satyr, recognizable by his particularly pointed ferine ears. In a relaxed pose of abandonment he rests his right elbow on a tree trunk. The entire figure is arranged on an oblique plane.

It is inclined on one side, according to the typical "Praxitelean" pose, with a branch acting as a strut. The right hand tightly holds a flute, and the right leg is bent and slightly positioned back. The left leg is straight, with the foot acting as a support. The left leg is counter-balanced by the arm held away from the body and the forearm rotated behind with the back of the hand resting on the left hip. The panther skin is arranged obliquely from the right

shoulder to the left hip. It also falls on the shoulders and back with rich folds formed by the knot placed at the height of the hip. Recent restoration revealed consistent remains of a yellow patina on the locks of hair, possible preparation for gilding. The sculpture is considered unanimously a copy of Praxiteles' *Anapauómenos* ("resting") Satyr, reproduced in numerous copies during the Roman period. They were utilized as villa decorations in small groves and fountains.

MUNIFICENTIA·SS·D·N·BENEDICTI
PP·XIV·A·D·MDCCLIII

Statue of the Albani Hermes-Antinous
The statue appears in the inventory of the Cardinal Albani in 1733 as "Antinous from Hadrian's Villa." Pope Clement XII acquired it for the recently constructed Museum. Recent restoration revealed that the reinsertion of the head, which accompanies the rhythm of the body, was executed with extreme care. The head inclines downward and is slightly rotated toward the right. The torsion of the neck and the tilt of the head with downward gaze are common of the iconography of Antinous.

Therefore, if it is not possible to catalogue the sculpture precisely as the youth deified after his tragic death, it is possible to hypothesize that the physiognomic features of the youth are similar to the representation of a divinity. The statue's provenience from Hadrian's Villa suggests that the emperor himself, a refined collector, commissioned the work to skillful artisans. These sculptors were active in Rome, and their products were clear interpretations of classical works. Understanding of this sculpture is unsure because of the absence

of qualifying attributes, the changed position of the arms, and the coexistence of themes and elements typical of the cultural syncretism of this period. These features also obscure the hand of the great author, whom many scholars identify as Praxiteles, Euphranor, or Polyclitus. In fact, a recent study recognizes the similarity between this sculpture and a bronze statuette representing Hermes (preserved in Paris at the Petit Palais), a Roman era replica of an original by Polyclitus ascribable to the first works of the Argive master.

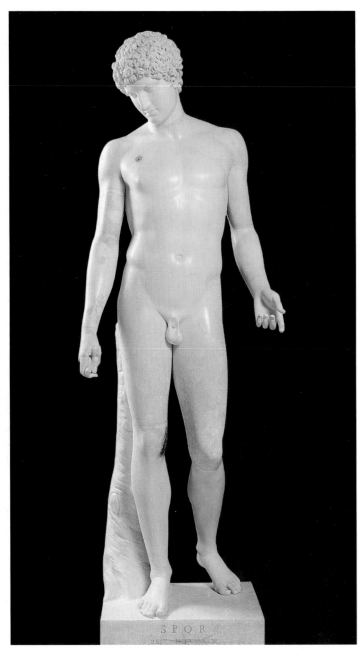

80

Capitoline Gaul

The sculpture, reproduced several times in engravings and drawings, is perhaps the most famous sculpture of the entire collection. In 1734, the statue was acquired from the Ludovisi Sculpture Collection. Probably the Ludovisi family found the statue on the premises of their villa. The Ludovisi villa was situated on the ancient *Horti* of Caesar, which through inheritance then passed into the possession of the historian Sallustius.

With great pathos the statue depicts a wounded Gaul (Galatian). His attributes are very evident: shield, *torques* around his neck, complete nudity, disordered locks of hair and moustache. The very visible wound indicates the sculptor's intention to depict the warrior in the last moment of resistance to his pain. Perhaps the image pertains to the great donation created during the era of Pergamon that Attalus placed along the terrace of the Temple of *Athena Nikephóros* in order to celebrate

his victories over the Galatians. It is possible that the Ludovisi statue group (today located in Palazzo Altemps) also belongs to Attalus' donation. Scholars do not agree on the date of this splendid sculpture. A recent hypothesis dates this copy to the Caesarian age. Another hypothesis asserts that the statue is a direct copy or the Pergamene original.

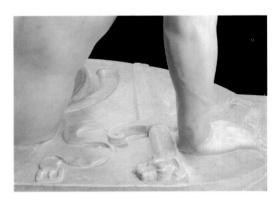

PALAZZO
DEI CONSERVATORI
CLEMENTINO
CAFFARELLI

Ground Floor

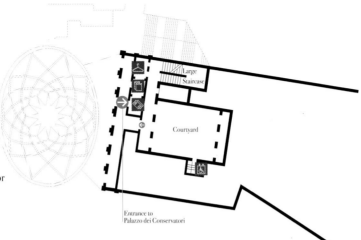

Ticket Office

Capitoline Bookstore

Checkroom

Handicapped-accessible elevator

First Floor

    I   Hall of the Horatii and Curiatii
   II Hall of the Captains
  III Hall of the Triumphs
  IV Hall of the She-wolf
   V Hall of the Geese
  VI Hall of the Eagles
 VII Green Hall
VIII Yellow Hall
  IX Pink Hall
   X Hall of the Tapestries
  XI Hall of Hannibal
 XII The Chapel
XIII XIV XV Halls of the Modern *Fasti*

Capitoline Bookstore

Handicapped-accessible elevator

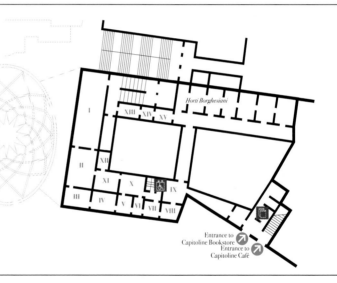

Second Floor

Picture Gallery
I II III IV V VI Halls
  VII Hall of Saint Petronilla
VIII Hall of Pietro da Cortona
   IX Cini Gallery

Capitoline Café

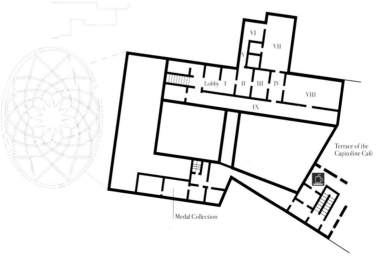

83

At least by 1363, the public statutes entrusted the seat of the public magistracy
to the Conservators. Their task was to assist the Senator in the governing
of the city. By the fourteenth century, the site had been occupied by the palace
of the Banderesi, captains of the public *militia* organized in "the satisfactory
partnership between crossbowmen and marines." Around the middle
of the fifteenth century, Pope Nicholas V commissioned the construction
of the palazzo (*"is summus pontifex* [...] *aliud (palatium) Conservatorum
a fundamenta construi* [...] *facit"*).
Images illustrating the Capitoline palaces before the transformation engineered
by Michelangelo show a building with a long portico with arches and columns
that houses the premises of arts and trade gilds. A continuous series
of cross-windows distinguished the upper part of the façade. The windows
provided light to the main rooms of the noble floor. Two loggias with double
lancet windows facing the piazza were located on the far ends of the palace.
Also a loggia with three arches delineated the façade facing the Campus Martius.
The courtyard, accessible through the portico on the piazza, was smaller than
the current one. (A document attests to the enlargement that took place in 1522).
On the right side, a series of ogival arcades characterized the courtyard.
The arcades were adjacent to another space, first site of the Capitoline
"statue collection." A staircase composed of a single flight led to the upper floor.
In 1563, Michelangelo began work, transforming the ancient palace,
still in its mediaeval phase, into a building of the classical nobility, according
to a "language" developed during his long experience with Roman architecture.
He completely changed the façade, locking it into a geometric scheme
of two orders: Corinthian, with gigantic pilasters that extend and divide the entire
structure, and Ionic, with columns that support the vaults of the portico.
Michelangelo proposed the same scheme of the façade for the courtyard,
on the side corresponding to the entrance. However, in this case, he emphasized
the division of the two orders. According to an ancient drawing, he arranged
the Consular and Triumphal *Fasti*, found in 1546 in the Roman Forum,
on the far wall. The transformation of the monumental staircase and the new
arrangement of the Conservators' Apartment effected the interior of the palace
so much that the early sixteenth century cycle of frescoes that decorated
the rooms facing the piazza was lost.

Under the pontificate of Clement XI (1720), Alessandro Specchi was the last
person to change the courtyard. He systematized the back wall that had been
stripped of the ancient *Fasti* fragments already for some time (1586)
and transferred to a room on the upper floor. Specchi, following the architectural
drawing of Michelangelo, deepened the portico to create a monumental space
to house the precious ancient sculptures just purchased from the Cesi Collection,
i.e., the seated goddess Roma and the colossal Barbarian figures made of *bigio
morato* marble.

On the right side of the Courtyard of the Palazzo dei Conservatori are the remnants
of the ogival arches that gave access to the room housing the "statue collection."
From the beginning of Capitoline collections of antiquity, the Courtyard
always has represented the privileged location as a sort of attraction for
the appropriation and preservation of the past. The works of art that gradually
came to the palace were tokens of the cultural continuity left by the ancient world,
a virtual bridge to a glorious past. The fragments of the colossal marble statue
of Constantine are located on the right side of the Courtyard.
These are different parts – head, hands, feet, and part of the arms – of the large
statue of the emperor. They were discovered in 1486 under the pontificate
of Innocent VIII in the western apse of the Basilica of Maxentius, finished
by Constantine, in the Roman Forum.
The statue represented the emperor seated on a throne, according to a model
relating to statues of Jupiter. It was constructed according to the acrolithic
technique; marble composed only the nude parts of the body, whereas drapery
of gilded bronze or even of stucco covering a supporting structure composed
the other parts. The head, of imposing size, depicts the sharply marked facial
features. The work dates between 313, the year of Constantine's dedication
of the Basilica, and 324, when the portrait of the emperor began to appear with
the diadem, the traces of which are visible on the marble.

Courtyard of the Palazzo
dei Conservatori
in the preceding arrangement

Courtyard of the Palazzo
dei Conservatori with
the fragments of the colossal
statue of Constantine

The reliefs of the Provinces and trophies of arms, originating in the Temple
of Hadrian in the Piazza di Pietra are on the left side of the Courtyard. Some
of the reliefs, counter-marked with the crests of the Conservators, were found
at the end of the sixteenth century, whereas, others were found in the same area,
beginning in 1883. The reliefs were located in the temple that Antoninus Pius
dedicated in AD 145 to his predecessor and foster father Hadrian,
who was deified upon death. The series of reliefs represents the personifications
of different provinces subject to the Roman Empire, recognizable by specific
attributes. Indeed, one of the characteristics of Hadrian's reign was his attention
given to the relationships with the various provinces. This aspect brought him
on long travels through the boundless extension of the Roman Empire.
Incorporated into the Palazzo della Borsa, the entire right side of the temple,
with eleven channeled columns capped by massive Corinthian capitals,
is preserved in the Piazza di Pietra.
The statuary group composed of the seated statue of Roma and the two Prisoners
in *bigio morato* marble is located on the far side of the Courtyard inside
the portico built by Alessandro Specchi. In 1720, Clement XI acquired
the statuary group from the Cesi Collection.
The group, already arranged in this form, was reproduced in ancient engravings
when it was located in the garden of the Cesi household, in the Borgo.
The central figure, representing a seated divinity derived from a model
of the Pheidian circle, was transformed into Roma with the addition of typical
attributes of this personification. The statue was placed on a base decorated
on the frontal part by a relief depicting a subjugated province, probably originally
part of the decoration of an arch dating to the first century AD.
The two colossal Barbarian figures, whose heads were added in the modern
period, are particularly precious because they are made of rare *bigio* marble.
They are comparable to the series of Dacian prisoners created for the decoration
of Trajan's Forum.

Four large historical reliefs originally decorating public monuments were
immured between 1572-1573 on the first landing of the large staircase. Before
the construction of the Picture Gallery, the landing was a small, open courtyard.
The first three reliefs were brought to the Capitoline Hill in 1515 from
the Church of Santi Luca e Martina. They are part of a series of eleven panels,
eight of which were reused for the decoration of the Arch of Constantine.
The original location of these reliefs is ascribable to official monuments
dedicated to Marcus Aurelius between AD 176 and 180. In 1573,
the Conservators purchased the fourth relief, originally located in a monument
dedicated to Hadrian and found nearby Piazza Sciarra, in order to complete
the decorative cycle.
The panel depicting Marcus Aurelius in the act of sacrificing in front of the
Temple of Capitoline Jupiter is located on the right, when ascending the stairs.
The emperor is depicted with a veiled head, pouring incense on a tripod. Next
to him stand the *camillus*, young assistant for sacrifices, a *flamen*, recognizable
by his characteristic hat, and a *victimarius*, ready to sacrifice a bull that appears
behind the group. The scene takes place before the Temple of Capitoline Jupiter.
This is one of the most detailed depictions of the temple, even though it appears
with four Corinthian columns instead of six due to spatial limitations.
The Capitoline triad appears in the pediment and a quadriga is located on the
peak of the roof.
The second relief represents a triumphal parade. The emperor, wearing a toga
and guiding a chariot led by four horses, is on the verge of passing through
a triumphal arch. A lictor and a flutist (*tibicen*) precede him. Behind, a small
winged Victory crowns the victorious general.
The relief depicting imperial clemency is located on the same wall. Riding
a horse, Marcus Aurelius is dressed in military garb with a breastplate
and *paludamentum*. He holds up his right hand, on the verge of bestowing his
clemency on two barbarians kneeling in front of him in a gesture
of submission. The pose of the emperor is very similar to the pose of the large
bronze statue located in the piazza, although in the statue in the piazza Marcus
Aurelius is depicted in civilian dress.
The fourth panel, originating in a monument built to honor Hadrian, depicts
the emperor entering the city (*adventus*), welcomed by the Genius of the Senate,

Relief from a monument
constructed in honor
of Marcus Aurelius:
the emperor makes a sacrifice
in front of the Temple
of Capitoline Jupiter

Relief from a monument
constructed in honor
of Marcus Aurelius:
the triumph of the emperor

Relief from a monument
constructed in honor
of Marcus Aurelius:
imperial clemency

the Genius of the People of Rome, and the goddess Roma. The goddess
is characterized by a short tunic, which reveals her right shoulder, and a plumed
helmet covering her head. Two other large historical reliefs, remnants from
the demolition of the so-called "Arco di Portogallo," and transferred
to the Capitoline Hill in 1664, decorate the other landings of the monumental
staircase. The Arco di Portogallo, located on the Via Lata (the current Via
del Corso), derived its name from its vicinity to the Portuguese Embassy. It was
a late-antique monument completely decorated with reused material.
It was destroyed in 1662 under the pontificate of Alexander VII in order
to enlarge the road.
The two Capitoline panels, originating in a monument in honor of Hadrian,
probably represent the only surviving elements of the decoration of the lost arch.
The first panel represents the emperor Hadrian presiding over a ceremony linked
with the distribution of food to Roman children.
The emperor is depicted on a high podium. The figures of the Genius
of the Senate and Genius of the People of Rome stand below him, in front
of the podium. In the foreground stands a child wearing a toga. On the possible
occasion of the reuse of the relief, the faces of the figures underwent important
recarving in order to be adapted to the new monument.
The second of the historical reliefs taken from the Arco di Portogallo was
arranged on the landing of the large staircase that leads to the Picture Gallery.
It represents the apotheosis of Sabina. Although unloved by her husband,
the emperor Hadrian, she became deified after her death. The emperor seated
on a chair assists in the apotheosis of Sabina, in the presence of the Genius
of the Campus Martius. Sabina rises from the funerary pyre, on the back
of a winged female figure identifiable as *Aeternitas*.
On the same landing are two beautiful panels in *opus sectile* representing tigers
attacking calves. They are two of the very few surviving elements
(another two smaller panels are preserved in the Palazzo Massimo at the Terme)
of the extraordinary marble decorations of the so-called "Basilica of Junius Bassus"
on the Esquiline. Junius Bassus, consul in AD 317, built the large hall.
Splendid polychromatic marble inlay entirely covered the walls of the large room.
After the destruction of the building, the precious wall decorations can be
reconstructed only through ancient drawings.

Relief from the Arco
di Portogallo: Hadrian presides
over the distribution
of food to Roman children

Relief from the Arco
di Portogallo: Hadrian assists
in the apotheosis of Sabina

Panel in *opus sectile*
with polychromatic marbles
from the Basilica of Junius
Bassus, representing a tiger
attacking a calf

The official rooms of the Palazzo dei Conservatori, the so-called "Apartment,"
have a particular character linked to the function of the areas that received
the magistracy of the Conservators, which played a central role in the municipal
structure beginning in the middle of the fourteenth century. This magistracy
was an expression of a municipal social class formed out of the public nobility
that possessed land in the outlying zones of the city and "bovattieri" (merchants)
enriched by the commerce in foodstuffs. The magistracy affirmed with pride its
autonomy (at least administrative), against the central power tied to the pontifical
Curia. The Statutes of the city of Rome, edited in 1363, recognized the power
of the Conservators in financial and economic matters. In fact, presiding over
the *Camera Urbis*, the Conservators administered and controlled customs
and public taxes. The Statutes also recognized the Conservators as a power
of control over the Senator who resided in the Palazzo Senatorio. In addition,
these statutes conferred on them the power to nominate other magistrates
and offices within the municipal structure. They were able to nominate
the leaders and the *magistri viarum*, who were entrusted with important tasks,
such as, respectively, the maintenance of public peace and provisions regarding
urban activities. The meetings of Public Council and Private Council attest
to the central role of the Conservators.
The representatives of the municipal social class and Capitoline magistracies
participated in these assemblies, conducted in the rooms of the Palazzo
dei Conservatori.
Nevertheless, the history and the importance of the role of the Roman
municipality is fully understood only in light of its relationship with
the pontifical Curia, of which the Governor of Rome was a member. This office,
created under the pontificate of Eugenius IV as direct issuing of papal power,
ended up depriving the Capitoline magistracy of its power.
In subsequent years, the Conservators lost their effective power and, although
continuing to exist, played a purely formal role for many centuries.
Nevertheless, beginning from the last decades of the fifteenth century,
with Sixtus IV's donation of bronzes in 1471, and the commission
of the first important cycle of frescoes in the official rooms in the first decade
of the sixteenth century, the Palazzo dei Conservatori underwent
a decorative and artistic renewal, culminating in Michelangelo's projects.

Hall of the Horatii and Curiatii.
Knight of Arpino,
Rape of the Sabine Women
(1636-1640)

Hall of the Horatii and Curiatii.
Knight of Arpino,
*Numa Pompilius institutes
the cult of the Vestals*
(1636-1640)

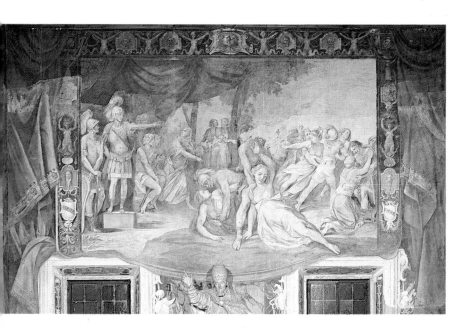

The halls of the Conservators' Apartment testify to the appeal to the ancient greatness of Rome, whose memory is exalted by the representation of examples of civil virtue. They contain important fresco cycles and are elaborately embellished with fine decorative elements, from engraved ceilings to sculpted or decorated doors, from stuccoes of the Chapel to eighteenth century tapestries of the Hall of the Tapestries, and to priceless ancient bronze statues which they contain. The commissioning of the oldest fresco cycle in the halls of the Apartment took place in the first decade of the sixteenth century. The commission chose for the theme of the cycle stories concerning the birth of the city and *exempla* of courage and virtue in the history of the Roman Republic. The frescoes in the Hall of Hannibal and the Hall of the She-wolf represent the only surviving elements of this cycle. The choice of subjects remained unchanged, even when the rooms assumed a new decorative cycle completed many years later in a definitely different historical and cultural context. The retention of the same theme confers a unitary character to the decoration of the halls of the Apartment and testifies to the endurance of the symbolic significance of the narrative elements through time.

Hall of the Horatii and Curiatii.
Knight of Arpino,
*Battle between the Horatii
and Curiatii* (1612-1613)

Hall of the Horatii and Curiatii.
Knight of Arpino,
Discovery of the She-wolf
(1595-1596)

The Public Council adjourned in the large hall, which assumed its current
dimensions following Michelangelo's restructuring of the palace.
Still today, it is the site of important ceremonies. For example, it was here that
the Treaty of Rome was signed in 1956, the first and founding act
of the European Union. In 1595, the painter Giuseppe Cesari, known
as the Knight of Arpino, was commissioned to create a new cycle of frescoes
in substitution of the preceding one, for the most part lost. Cesari, who worked
with the help of his workshop, conceived the cycle as tapestries hung along
the walls. On the short ends a heavy red curtain, held up by Telamones,
fell onto the scenes. On the long sides, vertical bands decorated with beautiful
garlands of fruits and flowers, trophies of arms, and lustral vases divide diverse
episodes. At the base extends a frieze in imitation marble with monochrome
medallions depicting episodes of Roman history related to the theme
in the fresco located above.
The Knight of Arpino referred to the stories of the birth of Rome and the first
kings narrated by the historian Titus Livy in his *Ab urbe condita libri*. In different
periods, the painter created the episodes of the *Discovery of the She-wolf*
(1595-1596), the *Battle against the inhabitants of Veii and Fidenae*
(1598-1601), and *the Combat of the Horatii and the Curiatii* (1612-1613).
There was a long interruption after the completion of these first frescoes.
They were not worked on again until 1636, and were completed in 1640, with the
creation of the last three episodes: *Rape of the Sabine Women, Numa Pompilius
institutes the cult of the Vestals*, and *Romulus sows the furrow of "Roma quadrata."*
Beginning in the second decade of the sixteenth century, statues of the popes
were placed in the room as clear recognition of papal authority.
Some of these statues were removed for various historical vicissitudes; only two
monumental sculptures remain. One is a statue of Urban VIII (1623-1644),
created by Bernini and his pupils between 1635 and 1640, and another,
in bronze in honor of Innocent X (1644-1655), created by Alessandro Algardi
between 1645 and 1650.
Today, in anticipation of the completion of the restoration of the museum,
two of the most prestigious works of art from the Capitoline collections,
the elements of the colossal bronze statue of Constantine and the gilded bronze
Hercules, are on exhibition in this room.

Gian Lorenzo Bernini:
(1598-1680) and helpers.
Pope Urban VIII (1635-1640)

Colossal bronze statue of Constantine
Beginning in the mediaeval period,
the precious remains of the sculpture
depicting the first Christian emperor
– the head, hand, and globe – were part
of the patrimony of the patriarch's Lateran
residence. In 1471, they went
to the Capitoline Hill, as part of Sixtus IV's
donation to the People of Rome.
The large head, a masterpiece of antique
bronze statuary, impressive both
in the colossal scale and the intensity
of the features, has been associated with

portraits of Constantine during the last
period of his life. The hand, intended
to hold up a globe, symbol of the power
over the world, is securely attributable
to the statue.

Gilded bronze statue of Hercules
The statue originated in the Forum Boarium, where it was found during the pontificate of Sixtus IV. The statue must have represented the cult statue within the round temple dedicated to the Greek hero in the second century BC. The statue's proportions and strong modeling demonstrate that it was based on Greek models of the fourth century BC, close to the Lysippic style.
A recent hypothesis suggests that it could have derived directly from the mold of a bronze statue of that period.

101

Between 1587 and 1594, painter Tommaso Laureti executed the decoration
of the fresco in the room. The fresco depicts the representation and exaltation
of the *exempla* of virtue and courage in the episodes of *Mucius Scaevola
and Porsenna, Horatius Cocles on the Pons Sublicius,* the *Justice of Brutus,*
and the *Victory at Lake Regillus,* following the narration of the Roman historian
Titus Livy. The Sicilian painter, summoned to Rome by Gregory XIII
to paint the ceiling of the Hall of Constantine, narrated the historical episodes
with monumental flare and lively colors. His pictorial language is full
of references to the paintings of Michelangelo. This is very clear in the details
of the fresco of *Mucius Scaevola and Porsenna.* In addition, there is not doubt
that the *Justice of Brutus* recalls the works of Raphael. This fresco, because
it is located in the room where the Conservators sat in the tribunal, acquires
a particular symbolic value.

Beginning in the last decade of the sixteenth century, this room, second for its
dimensions and the richness of the decorations only to the Hall of the Horatii
and Curiatii, was designated to celebrate, alongside the virtue of the ancient
ancestors, the wisdom of famous men and the valor of leaders of the Pontifical
State. Thus, funerary inscriptions were inserted in the walls. Among them,
the most noteworthy is the portrait created in memory of Virginio Cesarini
(1624), by either Bernini or Duquesnoy (opinions vary).

It is considered unanimously the most significant work of Roman sculpture
in the first decades of the seventeenth century. In addition, many statues in honor
of the Captains were located in the hall. To create these statues, ancient material
frequently was reused and reworked. For example, reuse is visible in the statue
in honor of Alessandro Farnese (in 1593, with the portrait by sculptor Ippolito
Buzi) and the colossal statue celebrating Marcantonio Colonna who,
at the command of the pontifical fleet, contributed to the victory of the Christian
armada in the Battle of Lepanto in 1571. In 1630, in order to honor
Carlo Barberini, brother of Urban VIII, the sculptor Alessandro Algardi
was entrusted with the restoration of a torso of a Roman cuirassed statue.
He completed the statue by adding legs and arms, in addition to a prestigious
shield. Bernini sculpted the portrait of the general with great efficacy.
Finally, there are two sculptures depicting Gianfrancesco Aldobrandini
and Tommaso Rospigliosi, by Ercole Ferrata.

Tommaso Laureti,
Justice of Brutus
(1587-1594)

Tommaso Laureti,
Victory at Lake Regillus
(1587-1594)

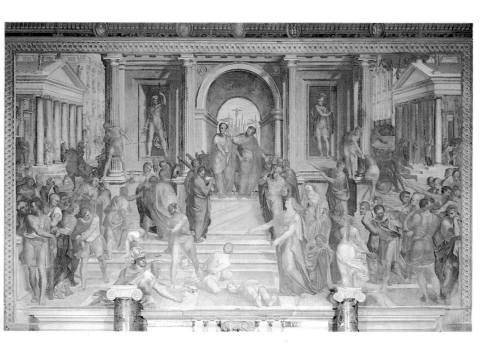

In 1569, when the external façade of the palace was still under construction,
painters Michele Alberti and Iacopo Rocchetti (or Rocca), pupils of Daniele
da Volterra, were commissioned to paint a frieze in fresco extending along
the length of the walls. The room derives its current name from this frieze.
It depicts the triumph of the consul Lucius Aemilius Paullus over Perseus,
king of Macedonia, held in 167 BC. The ancient historian Plutarch records
the episode with great detail. The painters narrated with vivacity and richness
the development of the conqueror's procession over the course of three days,
echoing the model of historical classical reliefs. The representation
of the consul's ascent to the Capitoline Hill (according to the ancient custom)
appears on the external wall that faces the city. However, the renewed façade
of the Palazzo dei Conservatori substitutes the Temple of Capitoline Jupiter,
as the final point of the triumphal procession, in an playful allusion recalling past
and present. Shortly before (1568), the carpenter Flaminio Bolonger completed
the wooden ceiling of the room. By recuperating the chromatic richness
of the wooden ceiling coffers, recent restorations restituted importance
to the prestigious engravings of the frames and of the beams and the finely
modeled trophies of arms located in the coffers.

Two paintings were commissioned for this room: the *Deposition*, by Paolo Piazza
in 1614 and *Saint Francesca Romana* by Giovanni Francesco Romanelli. In 1638,
the Conservators commissioned the latter work in honor of the patron saint
of the city. Pietro da Cortona executed another large painting in the room:
the *Battle of Alexander versus Darius*. According to the most recent study,
the painting was completed in the fifth decade of the seventeenth century in order
to celebrate Alessandro Sacchetti, commander of the pope's troops.

In this painting, the Tuscan painter demonstrates complete mastery of his art,
expressed with great skill and fluency.

Spinario
The small bronze statue, depicting a boy in the act of pulling a thorn out of his foot, was added to the Capitoline Hill in 1471, as part of Sixtus IV's donation of the Lateran bronzes to the People of Rome. The singular and particularly graceful pose of the figure, portrayed in an unusual position, made this work one of the most appreciated and copied during the Renaissance. At the same time, the unique pose of the statue created numerous questions regarding its identity.

It is an eclectic work, probably conceived in the first century BC, formed from Hellenistic models of the third-second century BC for the body, with a head derived from Greek works of the fifth century BC.

Camillus

Added to the Capitoline Hill through Sixtus IV's donation, this beautiful bronze statue is characterized by eyes in silver inlay. It was interpreted for many years as a Gypsy because of its soft and elegant hairstyle, feminine facial features, and dress softly draped over the body. The shape of the dress and comparison of this work with other statues suggest, instead, that this is a classical work of the first century AD. It depicts a youth responsible for a cult (*camillus*). The right hand once held a small cup used for ritual libations.

Capitoline Brutus
In 1564, Cardinal Pius da Carpi donated to the museum the magnificent bronze portrait of extraordinary expressive force. The identification of the statue with Junius Brutus, the first Roman consul, represents an astute interpretation of the antiquarian culture. However, this assertion is without any real foundation. Although the statue possesses features referable to Greek portrait models of poets and philosophers, a problematic understanding of the work of art suggests that it is the product of a powerful reinterpretation of the Roman artistic culture of the Republican age. Therefore, the statue dates between the fourth and third centuries BC. The extreme rarity of bronze portraits in this period, together with the possibility of such an ancient date, renders this work one of the most precious in the Capitoline collections.

Until the seventeenth century, the room was a loggia with three arches facing
the city. It was decorated with frescoes belonging to the first pictorial
embellishment of the Apartment of the Conservators. In the sixteenth century,
the presence of the She-wolf, among other sculptures, was documented
in this space. During research conducted in 1957, traces of the arches
were marked on the external wall. These constitute the only visible remains
of the loggia preserved today.

The frescoes generally are dated to the years 1508-1513. The insertion
of the Consular *Fasti*, first, and then the inscriptions honoring Alessandro
Farnese and Marcantonio Colonna (whose military exploits were celebrated
next to the Capitoline *Fasti*), irreversibly damaged the frescoes.

It is difficult to understand the frescoes because of their fragmentary condition.
The scene of triumph is identified as the *Triumph of Lucius Aemilius Paullus*,
and battle episode is identified as the *Campaign against the Tolostobogians*.
Following restoration of the entire room in 1865, a wooden coffered ceiling
was installed. It is still visible today. Recent restoration revived the decorative
vivacity of the ceiling. The background of the coffers contains pleasant,
quickly executed anthropomorphic forms interweaving with floral decorations,
an obvious referral to sixteenth century *grotesques*.

Detail of the coffered ceiling

Consular and Triumphal Fasti
They were discovered in the Roman Forum in the sixteenth century. The precious inscriptions originally decorated the Parthian Arch of Augustus, dedicated in 19 BC. The inscriptions, which represent irreplaceable documents for the understanding of Roman history, contain lists of the consuls from 483-19 BC and lists of triumphators from 753-19 BC. A precious fragment records the name of Romulus, founder of the city. Immediately after their discovery,

Michelangelo used the Capitoline *Fasti* as wall decorations on the back wall of the palace courtyard. In 1586, the *Fasti* were moved to their current location, with a systematization that recalls their arrangement in the courtyard.

Capitoline She-wolf

The statue is located in the center of the room, where in the sixteenth century Aldrovandi recalls that it was, "in a covered loggia that overlooks the urban plain." (The traces of the columns of the loggia are visible on the wall between the two windows.) The She-wolf, with its extraordinary evocative power, is the symbol of the city. The donation of Sixtus IV brought the statue to the Capitoline Hill. Initially, it stood in the fifteenth century façade of the palace. Then, it was transferred inside the palace, on the occasion of Michelangelo's architectural interventions. At that time, the twins were added. They transformed the ancient Lateran symbol of justice into '*Mater Romanorum.*' The creation of the work, which in origin probably had nothing to do with the legend of the origins of Rome, is attributable to a fifth century BC workshop in Etruria or Magna Graecia.

Recent restorations recuperated the pleasing decorative unity of the room
by freeing the sixteenth century ceiling from the cumbersome additions
and secondary paintings. In this way, the coffered ceiling acquired its original
"sky blue" color on the background where gilded decorations of fine
workmanship (rosettes of various forms, lustral vases, shields) are located.
The rediscovered colors harmonize well with the vivacious colors of the frieze
where elegant decorative elements alternating with trophies of flowers, fruits,
and weapons frame scenes depicting ancient games on the background
of real and fantastic landscapes. Among these is a view of the piazza
of the Capitoline Hill before Paul III Farnese's interventions (1534–1549) with
a faithful reproduction of the Church of the Aracoeli. Due to a lack of documents,
the fresco is associated with Paul III because of the lily of justice visible
on the shield. The work is attributed to various artists. According to the most
recent hypothesis, the artist belonged to the circle of Flemish artists active
in Rome in the third and fourth decades of the sixteenth century.
In the eighteenth century, the room was enriched by decorations of gilt stucco
to frame some works donated to the Capitoline and other works already located
in the room, for example, a copy of Francesco Penni's painting *The Holy Family*.
The statue of Medusa, placed on an ancient base, has been located in this room
since its donation to the Capitoline (1731). Notwithstanding different dates,
scholars have recognized unanimously that it is a work of Bernini.
Similarly, in the eighteenth century, a bronze portrait of Michelangelo on a bust
of *bigio* marble was donated to the Capitoline.

Gian Lorenzo Bernini
(1598-1680), *Medusa*

Bust
of Michelangelo Buonarroti

Bronze geese and vase with a bust of Isis
The room takes its name from the small bronze works, acquired by Pope Benedict XIII from the Carthusians of Santa Maria degli Angeli and donated to the Conservators in 1727. A precious architectural frame of stucco that encloses the group of works records the name of the donator. The bronze statues clearly recall the legend of the geese that sounded the alarm and saved the Capitoline Hill from the Gauls' invasion in 390 BC. Particularly interesting is the central piece, a bronze vase shaped like the bust of Isis.

Exquisitely rendered jewels decorate the figure of the goddess of Egyptian origin.

Crater of Mithridates Eupator
This splendidly decorated bronze vase placed in the center of the room evokes the sumptuous triumphal processions that took place in conclusion of wars of conquest in the East. During the procession, the most precious works of art taken from the enemy were put on display. In fact, an inscription engraved on the edge records the name of Mithridates VI, king of Pontus (120-63 BC). The vase arrived in Italy as Sulla or Pompey's spoil of war. The vase was found in Antium, in the Villa of Nero. Benedict XIV donated it to the museum in the eighteenth century.

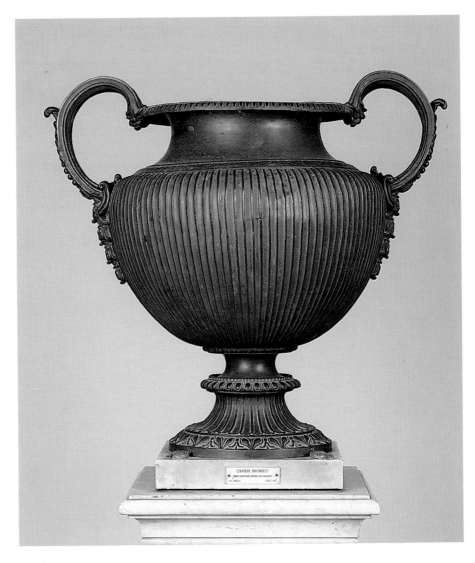

View of the Colosseum
(circa 1544)

The decoration of this small, refined room is contemporaneous with the decoration
of the preceding room. In the Hall of the Eagles, a frieze painted with prestigious
grotesques extends under the rich wooden ceiling where painted scenes alternate
with depressions decorated with gilded and engraved rosettes. Among the scenes
depicted in the frieze, the image of the Capitoline piazza is an interesting
document. It depicts the newly arrived equestrian statue of Marcus Aurelius
and the beginning interventions regarding the transformation of the palaces.

Green Hall

Table
The room contains two glass display cases housing a rich collection of ancient marbles. In the center of the room is a precious table decorated along the border with scenes from the life of Achilles. The work, which originally had a cult function, depicts in a continuous narrative cycle some of the most significant episodes from the life of the Greek hero, very popular in the fourth century BC. The original element was reutilized in the cosmatesque decoration from the Church of the Aracoeli. This decoration is a prestigious work of colored marble inlay that exalts the ingenuous but efficient figural ornamentation.

Yellow Hall

Ephedrismós
Two girls, one on the shoulders of the other, play *ephedrismós*, a game requiring teams, popular in Classical Greece. The unique position of the figures suggests a work of great complexity regarding the refined study of draperies and movement. Reworkings of this statue, conceived in the Hellenistic period, exist in terracotta and marble. The sculpture was found on the Esquiline in the vicinity of the *Horti Lamiani*.

Pink Hall

Busts of Roman emperors
The series of busts of Roman emperors and personages of the imperial age (Tiberius, Galba, Nerva, Hadrian, Marcus Aurelius, Clodius Albinus or Didius Julianus) come from the historical collections of the Capitoline Museums. The portrait of Hadrian in alabaster *verdognolo* represents a very significant work. Although its state of preservation is imperfect and the eighteenth century restoration gives its gaze a disturbing impression, the use of the rare Egyptian material and refined modeling identify it as a product of the highest level of the official court.

The room owes its current appearance to eighteenth century interventions.
In 1770, the room was renewed entirely to host the canopy (baldacchino)
of the papal throne.
Precious tapestries commissioned to the Roman factory of San Michele adorned
the walls. Thereafter, the doors were finely decorated and gilded. The doorframes
were made in colored marble (*diaspro* from Sicily). The painter Domenico Corvi
created the models for the tapestries. The subjects of the tapestries reproduced
works housed on the Capitoline Hill, e.g., Pieter Paul Rubens' painting
of the *Romulus and Remus suckled by the She-wolf* (which became part
of the Capitoline Picture Gallery) and the sculpture of the goddess Roma,
the so-called "Cesi Roma" (preserved in the courtyard of the Palazzo
dei Conservatori). The other two subjects also depict images that exalt the civic
virtues of the ancient ancestors: the *Vestal Tuccia* and the *Master of Falerii*.
Since 1544, according to the date recorded in a cartouche, the frescoed frieze,
depicting the life of Scipio Africanus, alternates with painted images of ancient
sculptures in the room. Traditionally, the fresco is attributed to Daniele
da Volterra, but more probably an artist from his circle created the work.
In the same years, a rich ceiling with hexagonal coffers with a blue background
was executed. The ceiling contains gilded engravings with helmets, shields,
and parade arms. The refurbished painted surface of the blue background
enhances the recent restoration of the precious gilding. The *consolles*
and the engraved and gilded wooden table, also dating to the eighteenth century,
contribute to the richness of the room.

Group of Commodus as Hercules flanked by two Tritons

The bust represents one of the most celebrated masterpieces of Roman portraiture. It depicts the emperor under the guise of Hercules. He wears Hercules' attributes: lion skin cap, club in the right hand, and apples of the Hesperides in the left hand, symbols of some of the Greek hero's Labors. The bust, extraordinarily well-preserved, rests on a complex allegorical composition composed of two kneeling Amazons (only one is preserved) flanking a globe decorated with zodiacal symbols. The Amazons hold up cornucopias that interweave around a pelta, the characteristic shield of the female warriors. The celebratory intent of the piece affirms the divine cult of the emperor through a language rich in symbols. The presence of the two marine Tritons flanking the central figure designates the statue as a sign of apotheosis. The group was found in a subterranean room from the complex of the *Horti Lamiani*, suggesting, probably, an attempt to conceal the figures.

Workshop of Iacopo Ripanda,
Hannibal in Italy
(circa 1508-1509)

The Hall of Hannibal is the only room that entirely preserves the original decoration of the frescoes from the Apartment dating to the first decade of the sixteenth century. Recent studies have cast doubt on the traditional attribution to the Bolognese painter Iacopo Ripanda. Although recognizing his presence on the Capitoline, indeed attested to by the literary sources, studies have not clarified whether the artist was the principal figure involved in the production of the fresco or a collaborator. The frescoes refer to the episodes of the Punic War and are framed by pilasters adorned with candelabra on a gold background. Under the scenes extends a frieze that was repainted many times. It depicts niches containing painted busts of Roman generals. The episodes, narrated with antiquarian taste, refer to the *Triumph of Rome over Sicily, Hannibal in Italy*, *Peace negotiations between Lutatius Catulus and Hamilcar*, and the *Naval Battle*, traditionally identified as the Battle of the Aegatians. Executed between 1516 and 1519, this wooden ceiling is the oldest ceiling in the palace. The seventeenth century inventories of the Apartment already documented noteworthy damage to the ceiling. Restoration has recuperated the elegant blue color of the background, reinvigorated by beautiful, gilded engravings. In particular, the representation of the twins with the She-wolf is very noticeable, given its position in the center of the cross vault.

After 1870, the Chapel of the palace was changed with the deconstruction
of the altar and the creation of a new door. Restructuring the Capitoline complex,
with the creation of new museum itineraries, allowed the reorganization
of the old chapel.

Now the environment is recomposed through the reinstallation of the altar
on the back wall. The altar is decorated with a rich frontal embellished with
precious colored marble inlay. Adorned with the bees of the Barberini crest,
the altar was executed under the pontificate of Urban VIII (1623-1644).
The original altar-piece, a slate that Marcello Venusti painted for the Capitoline
in 1577-1578, depicts *Mary between Saints Peter and Paul before the
background of Rome*. Between 1575-1578 Michele Alberti and Iacopo Rocchetti,
already active on the Capitoline, completed the fresco and stucco decorations
of the Chapel. The Chapel is dedicated to Mary and the protective saints
of the city, Peter and Paul. The frescoes inserted in the vaults illustrate
the episodes from the lives of the two saints.

The canvas paintings of the Evangelists and Roman saints attributed to Giovanni
Francesco Romanelli (1645-1648) complete the rich decoration of the Chapel.
Finally, the fresco of the *Madonna with Child and Angels* is attributed to Andrea
d'Assisi. Torn out from its original location in the ancient loggia of the palace,
it was transferred to the landing of the staircase. In the nineteenth century,
it was moved to cover the grate that allowed the Conservators and their entourage
to assist in the religious ceremonies from the Hall of the Captains.

Halls of the Modern *Fasti*

Statue of Marsyas

Greek mythology narrates that the Satyr Marsyas, who came to possess the flute of Athena, dared to challenge Apollo to a musical competition. With some contrivance, Apollo managed to win the contest, judged by the Muses, but he did not spare the Satyr, that dared to challenge a god, from a terrible revenge. Marsyas was flayed alive, and his skin was hung from a pine tree. A Roman copy of a Hellenistic original, this statue wisely exploits the particular veins of *pavonazzetto* marble to make the body seem flayed. The position of the figure has musculature in tension, and the face depicts a suffering expression. It is a true masterpiece of expressionistic art, and it offered much inspiration for many crucifixions.

For many years, restructuring efforts effected the entire museum complex and
resulted in the reopening of renewed spaces. Furthermore, they allowed
the addition of new exhibition spaces to the museum itinerary.

In particular, reorganization entailed Palazzo Clementino and Palazzo Caffarelli,
both of which compose, in reality, a singular property. In 1538, Ascanio Caffarelli
began construction on the land he received from Charles V. The palace arose
adjacent to the Palazzo dei Conservatori. Indeed, it directly faced the courtyard
of the public magistracy. The building expanded progressively and eventually
occupied a vast area of the Capitoline Hill. In 1584, an arch delimited
the entrance of the property facing the piazza, which one could reach through
the new Via delle Tre Pile. The name of Ascanio Gian Pietro Caffarelli adorned
the arch. In the meantime, new wings of the palace were under construction.
They were completed in 1680. At this point, the structure of a unique design
assumed its maximum extension by enclosing the small garden of the Palazzo
dei Conservatori (later called the Roman Garden), and by incorporating the large
space of the Caffarelli Garden.

At the beginning of the nineteenth century, part of this building was leased
to the ambassador of Prussia. Despite many attempts on the part of the Capitoline
authorities to take back these spaces, eventually the entire building became
property of the Prussians. In the meantime, the Prussian government had
acquired 20,000 square meters of the Capitoline Hill.

The Prussian presence on the hill came to an abrupt end at the end
of the First World War. In 1918, the Italian State expropriated the entire
property. Contemporaneously, demolition of the palace began, in order
to both distance the uncomfortable memory of the Prussian presence
in the palace and initiate archaeological surveys on the remains of the Temple
of Capitoline Jupiter. The highest floors of the eastern wing of the building,
where the "Hall of the Throne" was located, were destroyed in order to create
a vast terrace. In contrast, the ground floor was transformed into a new section
of the Capitoline Museums in record time. Named the Mussolini Museum,
it housed the most recent artifacts found in the urban area.

The rest is recent history. During the restructuring in this area of the museum
complex and removal of the pavement slabs in the Mussolini Museum
(later named the Museo Nuovo), the foundation structures of the Temple

of Capitoline Jupiter emerged in a good state of preservation. The enormous
temple foundation (55 m x 60 m) dates to the first phase of construction
of the sacred building in the sixth century BC. It was made with an imposing
structure composed of parallel divisions of *cappellaccio* blocks. This construction
goes through the level of clay on the surface of the hill and extends downward
to the layers of tufa. The large extension and good preservation of the foundation
structures, absolutely unexpected at the beginning of the excavation, were reused
entirely during the construction of Palazzo Caffarelli. Nothing remains
of the upper part of the temple. Its imposing mass of marble from the Republican
and imperial periods must have offered for centuries an inexhaustible quarry
of materials for sculptors and architects.

But the discoveries are not over, yet. A series of archaeological explorations were
conducted, preliminary to the construction of a large glass hall in the area
of the Roman Garden. At that time, the remains of a habitation were discovered,
dating to the earliest phases of life on the hill. The glass hall will constitute the
fulcrum of the new museum itinerary by housing the equestrian statue of Marcus
Aurelius. Only at the end of this delicate archaeological endeavor (in progress),
will it be possible to proceed in the completion of the roofing project.

The conclusion of this final project will close the cycle of the complex restoration
projects that are conferring a new aspect to the oldest museum complex of the world.

Roofing project
of the Roman Garden area
by Carlo Aymonino

Jacques Carlu, View of the
Capitolium dominated by the
Temple of Capitoline Jupiter
(1924)

Plan of the Temple
of Capitoline Jupiter in relation
to the complex of the palaces

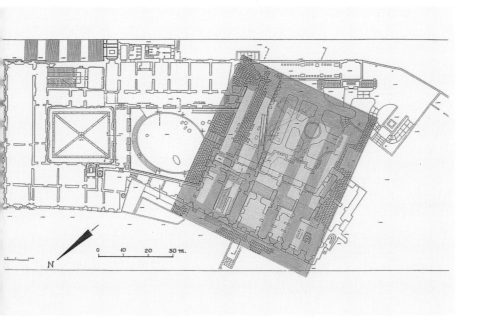

The Capitoline Medal Collection, constituted in 1872, contains numismatic, medal, glyptic, and jewelry collections of the Municipal patrimony.

The proclamation of Rome as capital of Italy brought about the upheaval of enormous extensions of territory in the city and a period of intense building activity. Afterward, followed the discovery of great amounts of archaeological material, ancient coins, and precious stones. The Archaeological Commission, instituted for the protection of ancient objects that were found in great quantities, oversaw the recovery of these materials by putting them in the collections of the Municipality of Rome. Thus, thanks to the fervent interest of some distinguished members of the Commission, the "Nummoteca", the numismatic collection within the rooms of the Capitoline Museums, was created.

Later, the same spaces housed the collections of the *Horti Lamiani*.

Before the annexation of Rome to the Kingdom of Italy, all numismatic material was housed in the Medal Collection in the Vatican and in the numismatic section of the Museo Kircheriano. In 1912, the latter became the Medal Collection of the Archaeological Superintendency of Rome, in Palazzo Massimo alle Terme.

The knight Augusto Castellani was the first director of the Capitoline Museums. Together with Rodolfo Lanciani, he was a member of the newly created Archaeological Commission. He was a passionate collector of antiquities and famous goldsmith. Through personal donations, Castellani saw to the formulation of a municipal numismatic cabinet. In fact, he gave 4,000 imperial coins, most of which were bronze asses and sesterces, found, for the most part, during his excavation of Portus.

He also gave a fine collection of late-imperial bronze coins, in addition to many silver coins dating to the twelfth and thirteenth centuries.

Augusto Castellani's fervent interest coincided with the fortunate circumstances surrounding a legacy from Kiev. The city of Rome inherited this collection, further stimulating the creation of the Capitoline Medal Collection. An Italian architect, Ludovico Stanzani, who lived and died in Russia, gave a noteworthy collection of ancient and modern coins (9,251) together with hundreds of cut stones. For this reason, at the end of October 1872, the Archaeological Commission decided to construct a numismatic room for a collection already containing over 5,000 coins.

The Stanzani Collection includes silver and bronze coins from the Roman

and Byzantine periods, in addition to a great quantity of gold, silver, and platinum
coins. These coins are Oriental, Russian, Polish, Swedish, and German.
The collection also contains a series of "bratteati" (bad money overlaid with gold
and silver) and several hundred precious and semi-precious cut stones.
Unfortunately, when the coins were registered in the Municipal Collection,
the provenience of the Roman and Byzantine coins was not recorded.
In 1873, after this legacy, the knight Castellani's numerous donations,
and the discoveries in these years, which oriented the Capitoline Collections
toward Roman numismatics, the Archaeological Commission acquired
the Campana Collection, stored for many years at the Monte di Pietà. Together
with some pieces preserved in Florence, the collection of the aurei of the
Capitoline Medal Collection constitutes the remains of the Gianpietro Campana's
Collection in Italy. He was an enlightened collector of rare and modern sensitivity
and patron of the arts and antiquity. He was also a very confident administrator
of the Sacro Monte di Pietà from 1833 to 1857, the year of his arrest
for embezzlement from the administration of the Monte. The passing of time and
better understanding of the papers and of the political-ecclesiastical environment
of the epoch cast serious doubts on the guilt of the Marquis Campana.
His presumed guilt led to the expropriation and subsequent dispersion abroad
of almost all of his rich collection.
The Campana Collection, containing 456 gold coins (aurei and solidi)
of the Roman and Byzantine periods, has extraordinarily well-preserved pieces.
The collection developed from a preexisting group of coins from the Albani
Collection that Campana received as inheritance from his father.
In 1897, the Archaeological Commission also acquired Giulio Bignami's
collection, consisting of more than 2,366 Republican coins for the Capitoline
Collections. This compilation enriched the Municipal Collection by relatively
completing the coin series of this period. Over a period of almost twenty years
of research, the collector had gathered many rare pieces from important
collections previously exhibited on national and international markets.
Thereafter, Bignami personally enriched the Medal Collection again through
a series of further donations.
In the first forty years of the twentieth century, the Capitoline Medal Collection
acquired some groups of coins found by chance. The following hoards became

part of the collection: a small treasure consisting of 1,371 mediaeval denarii
found nearby the Torre delle Milizie, a group of Republican denarii from the Area
Sacra di Largo Argentina, and a hoard of silver coins from the Capitoline Hill
piazza (maybe associated with a votive offering).

Finally, but no less important, was the fortuitous discovery of a treasure
of seventeen kilograms of gold coins and jewels during the destruction of an old
house. In fact, in February 1933, during the demolition of an old building
on the Via Alessandrina (which no longer exists due to the new systematization
of the area of the Fora and the creation of Via dei Fori Imperiali), a cascade
of gold coins poured out of a hiding place in an internal wall of a repossessed
house. Thereafter, a substantial cache of jewels was found in the same place.
The owner, Francesco Martinetti had concealed this treasure from his legitimate
heirs before his death in 1895. A versatile character who successfully participated
in the world of collecting in the nineteenth century, Martinetti was an antiquarian
restorer, jeweler, and forger. He collected, with great competency, the rarest and
best preserved Greek, Roman, Byzantine, Mediaeval, Papal, and modern coins
that were available on the market. Regarding the jewels found with the coins, he
was not interested in the creation of a collection. Instead, he gathered
the material only to satisfy the needs of collectors of that period. However, some
pieces of the collection originated in the Boncompagni-Ludovisi Collection.
The compilation became part of the collections of the Municipality of Rome only
in 1942, after a very long controversy involving Martinetti's heirs and the worker
who found the treasure. A very accurate assessment by a panel of specialists
resolved the situation.

Thereafter, the only other relevant additions to the Capitoline Medal Collections
were "Commendatore" Eugenio Di Castro's donation (Republican asses
and "madonnine" of Bologna), Baron Jordanov's donation, and some acquisition
made from the antiquarian market.

Next to the numismatic collections in the Capitoline Medal Collections, a small
part is dedicated to medallistics. It is composed of the Orsini Collection of seals
and medals, dating between 1330 and 1825, the collection of papal medals,
and a series of medals (mostly created by Lorenzo Lavy) from the Savoia
household. In addition, a series of commemorative medals (of various types)
belongs to this sector. Among these medals, the most interesting are those

depicting the standard of the Municipality in 1899 and in 1949, and the yearly
coinage of the three metals ordered by the Municipality of Rome from the State
"Poligrafico" (institution designated to publish public documents) in celebration
of the birthday of Rome.

A moderate assembly of glyptics and objects worked in gold belongs
to the Capitoline Medal Collections. The compilation is composed of specimens
originating from finds made throughout the city, inheritances, donations,
and acquisitions from the antiquarian market.

The Martinetti Collection is one of the most important glyptic collections.
It is composed of eighty-one objects worked in gold, with ancient and modern
gems. A large part of this collection once belonged to the Boncompagni-Ludovisi
Collection.

Regarding jewelry, a noteworthy piece is the Senator's necklace with a large
medallion composed of a tiny mosaic. Augusto Castellani made it in 1869
for the last Senator of Rome, the Marquis Francesco Cavalletti Rondinini.
Two *demi-parures* made by Castellani are also interesting. Umberto Speranza
donated them in 1976 in memory of his wife Giannina Fabri Speranza,
the last direct descendant of Augusto Castellani. The two *parures*, one in gold,
the other in gold and pearls, are a perfect demonstration of the eclectic repertoire
of the Castellani goldsmiths. They were inspired so much by Classical, Christian,
and Renaissance arts that they attempted to experiment with ancient techniques
of granulation and filigree (sometimes together with tiny mosaics).

Gold brooch with mounting of embossed work from which hang two long chains terminating in small ivy leaves.
The mounting contains an amethyst engraved with a griffin attacking an ibex. It is probably a work of Eastern artists, dating to the first century BC. It comes from the outfit of *Crepereia Tryphaena*. It was found in 1889 in a tomb dated to the second half of the second century AD, during construction of the Palace of Justice in the Prati quarter.

Eagle-shaped Gothic *fibula* made of a gold foil covered in silver. Tiny gold sheets and garnets are applied to the gold foil through the *cloisonné* technique.
The eyes are composed of garnets inserted into semicircular rock crystals. They were found in a burial on the Via Flaminia datable to the end of the fifth and the sixth century AD.

Collection of sulfur casts representing some of the gems from the Boncompagni-Ludovisi Collection. Purchased by the "Friends of the Museums" for the Capitoline Medal Collection.

Necklace of the Senator made by Augusto Castellani in 1869 for the last Senator of Rome, the Marquis Francesco Cavalletti Rondinini. It was created with 47 emeralds, 62 rubies, and 76 sapphires. It was commissioned in order to substitute the old necklace, whose medallion represented senatorial authority. Senator Cavalletti wore the necklace only for a few months because on September 20, 1870 he had to consign it to the first public council.

The minute-mosaic medallion of the Senator's necklace made by Luigi Podio, "mosaicist" of Castellani. On the front, the crest of the Roman Senate with a crown on top. On the reverse, the inscriptions *PIO P(a)P(ae) NONO* and *INSTAURATORI*, referring to the magistracy's reform in 1847.

Gold ring with engraved aquamarine that represents Neptune in the middle, guiding two tritons on the waves of the sea. Beneath, KY·INTIΛ (*Quintillus*). Initially in the Boncompagni-Ludovisi Collection, then the Martinetti Collection. Probably dates to the sixteenth century.

Gold medallion with cameo in sardonyx with fracture restored in gold. Represents two facing busts. One figure wears the *pallium*; the other has a hairstyle typical of the third century AD. Previously interpreted as an imperial couple. Instead, probably the medallion represents a private married couple. Martinetti Collection.

Quinarian aureus of Augustus. Unique coined specimen, probably in the mint of the *Colonia Patricia* or the mint of Nîmes between 18 and 16 BC. Probably related to the restitution of the military standards that Crassus lost in the battle of Carrhae. Martinetti Collection.

Solidus of Valentinian III
(Flavius Placidus Valentinian),
AD 425–455. Campana Collection.

Aureus of Claudius. On the reverse,
depiction of the interior of the Praetorian
camp, AD 41–43. Campana Collection.

Sesterces of Trajan. On the reverse,
depiction of the Circus Maximus in order
to record the emperor's great building
efforts, AD 113.

The creation of the Capitoline Picture Gallery represents one of the most
significant and famous examples of the pontifical government's patronage
in the eighteenth century. The Picture Gallery is the result of Pope Benedict
XIV's intelligent, cultural policy, focused on the defense of the Roman artistic
patrimony. Cardinal Silvio Valenti Gonzaga, Secretary of State and a famous
collector, skillfully exploited the possibility of purchasing two of the most
significant Roman collections. They belonged to the marquises Sacchetti
and the Pio princes. The cardinal acquired these collections by sustaining
the importance of their protection (in order to prevent the dispersion of the two
prestigious collections) and by sustaining that they were didactic instruments.
In fact, the School of the Nude of the Academy of San Luca was established
on the Capitoline Hill with the Picture Gallery. This school allowed young artists
to study directly works from the past.
The Sacchetti had to sell a conspicuous part of their noteworthy collection
of paintings in order to pay their creditors. Valenti Gonzaga conducted
the negotiations and on January 3, 1748 acquired 187 paintings. A short time
later, Prince Giberto Pio asked the pope for permission to transfer the family
collection of paintings to Spain (with the obvious intention of selling it).
The pope authorized the prince, under the condition that the pope could choose
some of the paintings. By doing so, he demonstrated his firm intent to impede
the departure of a conspicuous number of paintings from Rome. Therefore,
in 1750, the prince had to yield to the pope a fourth (i.e., 126 paintings)
of his collection. The current Halls of Saint Petronilla (Sacchetti) and of Pietro
da Cortona (Pio) were built specifically to house the two collections.
In 1818, some adjustments were made on the original collection dating
to the middle of the eighteenth century, according to the decision to move
to the Capitoline collections the large altar-piece with Guercino's *Burial of Saint
Petronilla*. Its arrival necessitated the relocation of some works of art
of the Capitoline collections to the Vatican Picture Gallery and the Academy
of San Luca. Some important acquisitions made between the nineteenth
and twentieth centuries compensated for the loss of these works. Among the new
purchases is a small but precious group of paintings on wooden panels dating
to the fourteenth and fifteenth centuries, originally in the Sterbini collection.
Thanks to some donations, the patrimony of the Capitoline collection also

currently consists of important, valuable groups of decorative and applied art. They are the Cini legacy of porcelain and Roman furniture of the seventeenth century, the legacy of Primoli, consisting of paintings and furniture of the eighteenth century, and finally, the Mereghi donation of porcelain from the Far East. In the last decades, other donations and remarkable purchases have contributed to enrich the nature of the Picture Gallery.

Pierre Subleyras,
Portrait of Cardinal
Silvio Valenti Gonzaga

Central Italy from the Mediaeval to the Renaissance

The room contains paintings on wooden panels, dating from the late mediaeval
to the sixteenth century. They attest to the major changes that took place
in Italian painting from the fourteenth century onwards. The subject of these
works of art is almost always religious. In addition, different formats
of the paintings demonstrate the variety in production. In the case
of the mediaeval paintings, there are several examples of fragments of polyptychs
(works of large dimension designated for altars). In these works, images of saints
or famous episodes from religious history frame the central panels dedicated
to Christ or Mary. Such is the case of the *Magdalene* and *Saint Bartholomew*
by Bartolomeo Bulgarini of Siena (cited between 1337 to 1378). In comparison,
the Florentine painting on a wooden panel, *Coronation of Mary*, was probably
the upper part (cyma) of a far vaster composition. Sixteenth century works
demonstrate how rapid the diffusion of pictorial novelties of the early Renaissance
was in different Italian cities.

Nicholas of Pietro Gerini (Florence, cited between 1368 and 1416), *Trinity*. The work was made for the merchant from Prato, Francesco Datini, depicted with his wife in the lower part of the painting. He is recognizable by his coat of arms. The overt lack of proportion was a desired effect, as a sign of humility before divine personages.

Cola dell'Amatrice (Nicola Filotesio, Amatrice 1480 - Ascoli Piceno around 1547), *Death and Assumption of Mary*. It was originally in the Church of San Domenico in Ascoli Piceno. The subject, transmitted by the apocryphal writings, was very diffuse, and the Dominican order was committed to the propagation of the cult of Mary.

Francesco Francia (Bologna 1450 - 1517) and Bartolomeo Passerotti (Bologna 1529 - 1592), *Presentation at the Temple*. The painting, initiated by Francia (probably for a church in Bologna), has the classic shape of an altar-piece. With the death of the artist, the piece remained unfinished. Years later, Passerotti completed the painting, with some modifications, including the transformation of the client, kneeling on the right, into a depiction of Saint Jerome with the lion.

The sixteenth century at Ferrara

Ferrara was a lively cultural town (it is enough to consider Ludovico Ariosto
and Torquato Tasso) and the capital of the seigniory of the Estensi. In 1598,
the Church annexed the city. Due to the town's geographical position,
the paintings from Ferrara are characterized by a combination of Venetian artistic
preferences, based on a bright chromatic scale, and a soundly composed design,
characteristic of central Italian production. Direct analysis of the works of Titian
and Raphael enabled the main artists from Ferrara to paint works with great
evocative charm and attention to detail. The presence of well-established
workshops – Garofalo's was the main one – contributed to the dissemination
of sophisticated discernment.

Garofalo (Benvenuto Tisi, Garofalo circa 1476 - Ferrara 1559), *Annunciation*. The date 1528 is legible on the right and above the fireplace. The three carnations in the foreground are an overt reference to the artist's nickname. The magnificence of the Archangel Gabriel's garments contrasts with the simplicity of Mary, depicted in domestic intimacy. The diagonal constituted by the three figures of the Trinity (the Father, Infant Jesus with the symbols of the Passion, and the dove of the Holy Spirit), cuts across the solid spatial structure of the painting, enhanced by the central columns.

Dosso Dossi (Giovanni Luteri, ? circa 1489 - Ferrara 1542), *The Holy Family*. The great altar-piece was painted around 1527 for a church of Ferrara. The altar-piece draws attention to the loving relationship (depicted with lively, naturalistic emphasis) among Mary, the Infant Jesus, and Saint Joseph. Mary's graceful pose derives from a solid, imposing structure, enhanced by the balanced, colored nuances of her garments.

Scarsellino (Ippolito Scarsella, Ferrara circa 1550 - 1620), *Adoration of the Magi*. The painter was the last protagonist of the most important artistic period in Ferrara. This circa seventeenth century canvas recalls the artistic tradition of Ferrara, as much as that of Venetian painting and the new Bolognese motifs. The Holy Family is depicted in an architectural setting, rather than in the usual stable.

Venice and its territory: the sixteenth century

The Turkish conquests and the discovery of America caused the abrupt
interruption of Venice's well-established commercial relationship with the East.
Therefore, the Venetian State (the Serenissima Repubblica) directed its interests
toward Italy, with obvious consequences on its artistic production. In a short
time, Venice became, together with Florence and Rome, one of the main painting
centers. The particular emphasis on colors is the principal characteristic
of Venetian paintings. Thanks to the extended production of the workshops
of Titian, Tintoretto, Veronese and Bassano, Venice greatly influenced all
of European painting until the middle of the eighteenth century.

Tiziano Vecellio (Pieve di Cadore circa 1490 - Venice 1576), *Baptism of Christ*. Early work (circa 1512). It was commissioned for Giovanni Ram, depicted on the right. He observes the evangelical episode.

Giovanni Girolamo Savoldo (Brescia circa 1480 - Venice 1548), *Portrait of a woman*. The art of the inland part of Veneto combined artistic motifs of the lagoon city with traditional realism of Lombard painting. The woman, whose sober elegance and devotion are evident (note the small prayer book in her left hand), is depicted with a small dragon, the symbol of Saint Margaret, patroness of women in labor.

Veronese (Paolo Caliari, Verona 1528 - Venice 1588), *Rape of Europa*. The mythological subject, particularly dear to the painter, is well known. Jupiter, in the guise of a white bull, carries the young Europa to the island of Crete. The canvas depicts the full range of the artist's extraordinary scenographic skill through his use of a vibrant color spectrum.

Between the sixteenth and seventeenth centuries: Emilia and Rome

The works in this room, mostly from Emilia, are a precious record of the variety
in artistic production. Contemporary with great works commissioned
for churches and public and private palaces, works of lesser dimensions were
designated for smaller spaces as well as copies of famous works that were very
requested by the market. Paintings of this genre had a very important role
in the diffusion of new artistic motifs and enabled many generations of young
painters to study the works of the great masters.

Copy by Correggio (Antonio Allegri,
Correggio 1494 - Parma 1534),
Madonna of Albinea.
The original, lost in the eighteenth
century, was created for the Church
of San Prospero in Albinea
(Reggio Emilia). Correggio is one
of the most important protagonists
of the early sixteenth century.
In the seventeenth century, his classical
style became a reference point for the great
Emilian painters.

Knight of Arpino (Giuseppe Cesari,
Arpino 1568 - Rome 1640),
Diane the Huntress.
The uncommon narrative skill
of this painter, who created this small,
sophisticated painting on a wooden
panel around 1600, can be understood
better through the frescoes in the Hall
of the Horatii and Curiatii, located
on the first floor of this building.

Hall
of Saint Petronilla

The Capitoline
Picture Gallery

Palazzo
dei Conservatori

The great paintings of the seventeenth century in Rome

The name of this room derives from the title of Guercino's work. The piece
is over seven meters tall. It depicts the *Burial of Saint Petronilla*. It was
commissioned for an altar in Saint Peter's Basilica. In 1818, it was transferred
to the back wall of this room.

The room contains works of extraordinary importance, such as Caravaggio's
two works, *Good Luck* (circa 1595) and *Saint John the Baptist* (circa 1602),
and other significant examples of the first decades of the seventeenth century
directly or indirectly linked to Roman painting production. Rome was the main
center of illustrative culture and the meeting place of artists of different origins,
at least until the middle of the seventeenth century. At the end of the sixteenth
century in Rome, two new events took place, destined to revolutionize the field
of figurative arts. In the early 1590s, Michelangelo Merisi da Caravaggio arrived
in Rome from Lombardy and in 1595 Annibale Carracci arrived in Rome from
Bologna. Carracci was commissioned to fresco the gallery of the Palazzo Farnese.
In different ways, the two artists deeply influenced the meaning of pictorial
research. Caravaggio directed attention toward reality. Annibale directed
attention toward a new classicism deeply meditated on ancient examples
and the work of Raphael. Domenichino was a direct pupil of Annibale,
and he soon played a key role in Rome as the leader of the classical mode.
The *Sibyl* of circa 1622 echoes the idealized models of the Raphaelesque matrix.
Francesco Albani (Bologna 1578-1660) comes from the school of Annibale.
In Bologna, around 1610, before his transfer to Rome, he created a large canvas
painting of the *Birth of Mary* and a painting on slate of *Mary with the Child
and Angels*, proof of his mature classicism. The remarkable group of paintings
by Guercino allows one to follow the various phases of his rich production.
Saint Matthew and the Angel numbers among his first period masterpieces.
At that time, his early style was characterized by shaded contours and by dense
and fluid material. Once he returned to Emilia, Guercino turned towards
a more firm and classical style, as *Cleopatra before Octavian* and the *Persian
Sibyl* demonstrate.

Caravaggio (Michelangelo Merisi,
Caravaggio 1571 - Porto Ercole 1610),
Good Luck.
It is an early work, created around 1595
as part of Cardinal Francesco Maria
Del Monte's collection. The cardinal
was one of the artist's first patrons.
The subject of the painting reveals
Caravaggio's new interest in scenes taken
from the street. Equally new is the
presentation of the protagonists, depicted
against a clear background, without any
indication of environment or depth.

Caravaggio (Michelangelo Merisi,
Caravaggio 1571 - Porto Ercole 1610),
Saint John the Baptist.
Painted around 1602 for the Mattei family,
the work seems revolutionary for two
reasons. First, the saint is represented
in a new pose (although it was inspired
by Michelangelo's *ignudi* on the Sistine
Chapel). Second, the use of *chiaroscuro*
(light and dark effects) makes the figure
powerfully emerge from an indistinct
background.

Pieter Paul Rubens (Siegen 1577 - Antwerp 1640), *Romulus and Remus*.

The canvas painting was created in the middle of the second decade of the seventeenth century in Antwerp, where the artist settled upon his return to Italy. In fact, Rubens was one of the first foreign artists in the seventeenth century that had a long, fruitful Italian experience from 1600 to 1608.

In the painting, the central group derives from an ancient sculpture of the She-wolf and the twins next to the Tiber River. The artist saw and drew this sculpture group in the Vatican.

Guercino (Giovanni Francesco Barbieri, Cento 1591 - Bologna 1666), *Burial of Saint Petronilla*. The large altar-piece was painted for Saint Peter's Basilica between 1621 and 1623. Gregory XV Ludovisi, the Bolognese pope who called the artist to Rome, commissioned the work. The work is divided into two registers. At the bottom, the powerful figures of the gravediggers lower the saint into the tomb. They are surrounded by other groups of well-defined personages in the background. Above, the apotheosis is rendered through the contrast between the beautiful figure of Christ and the rich, decorated garment of the saint.

Paintings in Bologna from the Carracci to Guido Reni

The room contains works from the Bolognese school created between the end
of the sixteenth century and the first half of the seventeenth century. Some
of these works are important examples of the religious images tied to the new
spirit of the Counter-Reformation that was codified in the artistic field through
the *Discourse about sacred and profane images* by Cardinal Gabriele Paleotti
(the bishop of Bologna). In the same years, the Bolognese Academy, founded
by Annibale and Agostino Carracci and their cousin Ludovico, progressively
developed a type of devotional art attentive of this new, profoundly religious
sensitivity. This is visible in Annibale's *Saint Francis Adores the Crucifix*
(circa 1585) and Ludovico Carracci's painting of the same subject (Bologna,
1555-1609), *The Holy Family and the Saints* (circa 1590), and the small canvas
painting of *Santa Cecilia* (1603-1605).
Many of Guido Reni's paintings and those related to his close circle are on display
in this room. The artist, who arrived in Rome in 1599, had attended the academy
of the Carracci. Later, he preferred to return to Bologna to pursue his form
of classicism. Guido Reni's research of the ideal beauty finally reached a picture
free of any attempt to imitate the external reality, as his last works displayed
in this room attest: *Blessed Soul, Girl with a Crown, Lucretia, Cleopatra*,
and *Jesus and Saint Giovannino*.

Guido Reni (Bologna, 1575 - 1642),
Saint Sebastian.
The work is datable around 1615.
The saint is depicted in the foreground,
against a landscape animated with small
figures. The body of the saint clearly
imitates classical statues that the artist
studied in Rome.

Guido Reni (Bologna, 1575 - 1642)
Blessed Soul.
Painted in 1640-1642, it was located
in the artist's study at the time of his death,
according to the inventory of goods.
Here, the religiousness of Guido found
expression in a pure, abstract image
that depicted the soul ascending
into heaven toward the divine light.
The beauty of the nude, which rests
on the curve of the globe, echoes ancient
models.

Guido Reni (Bologna, 1575 - 1642),
Girl with a Crown.
It is difficult to identify the figure in this
painting. Without a doubt, it is one
of the most exceptional final works
of this artist. The pose and the drapery
of the garments are based on an ancient
sculpture. The image embodies Reni's
last paintings with evocative power.
Agile brushstrokes and the absence
of color make this figure seem almost
without substance.

Baroque paintings: Pietro da Cortona and his circle

Baroque was born around the 1630s, out of the intense Roman cultural
environment of the first decades of the seventeenth century. The term "Baroque"
is generic and defines a complex derivation from classicism. The main season
of Baroque coincides with the papacy of Urban VIII Barberini. He personally
was involved in the programmatic selection of artists and remarkable urban
and decorative enterprises. The exceptional career of Gian Lorenzo Bernini
as a sculptor and architect corresponds to Pietro da Cortona's painting
endeavors. Da Cortona was the first authentic representative of the new style.
The room contains a significant number of Pietro da Cortona's works
commissioned for the Sacchetti family, beginning with the first period of his
extended stay in Rome. In 1612, the artist departed from his native Tuscany
and arrived in Rome, where, later, he became head of an important workshop.
Giovanni Maria Bottalla (Savona, 1613-1644), follower of Pietro, produced
two large paintings of biblical content: *Meeting between Esau and Job*
and *Joseph Sold by his Brothers*, completed around 1640. Giovanni Francesco
Romanelli (Viterbo, 1610-1662), one of Pietro's greatest pupils, painted
the *Rape of Helen* in circa 1631, and the very beautiful *David* in circa 1640.
The latter attests to his definite autonomy from his master's style, in favor
of a refined, personal classicism.

Pietro da Cortona (Pietro Berrettini, Cortona 1597 - Rome 1669), *Sacrifice of Polyxena*.
The work is dated around 1624. It represents an important attempt in the creation of paintings of large dimensions. The dramatic subject of the Trojan heroine, Priam's daughter, was derived from successive reworkings of Homeric poems. The scene is composed of three groups of figures symmetrically distributed and lined up parallel to the background. A nocturnal light illuminates a background full of barely visible trees and architecture. The consistency of the painting material is exceptionally thick.

Pietro da Cortona (Pietro Berrettini, Cortona 1597 - Rome 1669), *Rape of the Sabines*.
The episode, narrated by Plutarch and Titus Livy, depicts the legendary origins of Rome. The artist represented the scene in a way entirely different from the *Sacrifice of Polyxena*. Here, symmetry is abandoned in favor of dynamic and centrifugal movement, and the entire composition is based on diagonal lines. Pietro da Cortona reaches his stylistic maturity in this work.

The painting, completed in circa 1630, rightly is considered the first "manifestation" of Baroque painting.

Pietro da Cortona (Pietro Berrettini, Cortona 1597 - Rome 1669), *Portrait of Urban VIII*.
The Sacchetti family's social status increased through the nomination of Maffeo Barberini (named Urban VIII) for the papacy in 1623. This painting, executed around 1626-1627, attests to the fellowship between the Barberini and Sacchetti families. They commissioned Pietro to paint a portrait of their protector.

Artistic trends in Rome during the seventeenth century

This room contains works that compare with those in the Halls of Saint Petronilla, Pietro da Cortona, and the Cini Gallery. The exhibited works date between the third and sixth decades of the seventeenth century. They are ascribable to the intense period of Roman Baroque art production.

As already mentioned Rome was a place of meeting, formation, and study of artists from different places during the first half of the seventeenth century. For example, the French François Perrier executed two paintings of biblical content: *Moses Draws Water from the Rock* and *Adoration of the Golden Calf*. From Ticino, Pier Francesco Mola created *Diane and Endymion*. From Emilia, Giovanni Lanfranco was commissioned to paint *Erminia among the Shepherds*, and Emilio Savonanzi created the *Death of Adonis*. Some small paintings attest to the taste developed in the first period of the seventeenth century for the ideal landscape genre. The highest expression of this genre occurs in the works of Annibale Carracci and Domenichino. Giovanni Battista Viola and Pietro Paolo Bonzi, who painted works displayed in this room, became specialists in this trend.

François Perrier (Selins 1590 - Paris 1650), *Adoration of the Golden Calf*. Around 1641-1642, Cardinal Giulio Sacchetti commissioned this painting together with the companion piece of *Moses Draws Water from the Rock*. The artist reworked figures created by the most important masters of the epoch, especially Pietro da Cortona and Poussin, in the execution of these two monumental paintings. In these works, the complexity of the composition accompanies the refined chromatic study.

Pier Francesco Mola (Coldrerio 1612 - Rome 1666), *Diane and Endymion*. Around 1660, Bonaventura Argenti, musician of the Papal Chapel, commissioned the work. A romantic atmosphere permeates this nocturnal scene. The moon (Diane) looks down upon the shepherd Endymion, who sleeps. Jupiter gave him eternal sleep in exchange for eternal youth. Mola is one of the most famous representatives of the neo-Venetian trend, evident in this work.

This room derives its name from the legacy (in 1880) of the Roman count
Francesco Cini. He donated his rich collection of porcelain and furniture
to the Municipality of Rome. In the different sectors of the gallery, the paintings are
clustered according to genre. Next to the *exedra* with the glass display cases
containing Chinese porcelain are displayed Flemish and Dutch works:
the *Crucifixion* by Gabriel Metsu (Leida 1629 - Amsterdam 1667), the *Triumph
of the Cross* by Leonard Bramer (Delft 1596 - 1674), and some small landscapes.
These panoramic scenes attest to the diffusion of this particular pictorial genre
in northern Europe. The works displayed on the left wall before the columns
belong to the paintings of this genre. *Farmers* by Michael Sweerts (Brussels 1618
- Goa 1664) and *Dance of the Farmers* by Michelangelo Cerquozzi (Rome 1602
- 1660) demonstrate the new attention to scenes of daily life and simple people.
The *Witch* and *Soldier* by Salvator Rosa (Naples 1615 - Rome 1673) date to
the middle of the seventeenth century. Gaspar Van Wittel's (Amersfoort 1653
- Rome 1736) ten works belong to the genre of "vedutismo" (city views). It spread
in the eighteenth century. Van Wittel's series of seven *Views of Rome* executed
in tempera colors on pergamene parchment is especially prestigious. The next
space contains a significant series of portraits painted between the fifteenth and
seventeenth centuries. The two small works by Giovanni Bellini (Venice circa 1432
- 1516) and Giovanni Buonconsiglio, nicknamed Marescalco (Vicenza circa 1470
- 1535/1537) constitute significant examples of Venetian portraiture in the late
fifteenth century. The three paintings by Bartolomeo Passerotti (Bologna 1529
- 1592) depict an emphasized psychological introspection. He is one of the most
famous portrait artists of the sixteenth century. His *Portrait of a Man*, *Portrait
of a Man with a Dog*, and *Double Portrait of Musicians* are works datable between
the end of the 1570s and 1585. The two portraits of Anton Van Dyck and
the problematic portrait attributed to Diego Velázquez are prestigious examples
of seventeenth century portraiture. The last area of the Cini Gallery is dedicated
to the small group of eighteenth century works. Domenico Corvi (Viterbo 1721
- Rome 1803) painted *Romulus and Remus*, a copy of Rubens' painting,
(today housed in the Hall of Saint Petronilla), the *Enthroned Goddess Roma*,
the *Vestal Tuccia*, and *Camillus and the Pedagogue of Falerii*. These preparatory
works were commissioned in 1764 for the tapestries conserved in the Hall of
the Tapestries in the Apartment of the Conservators. *The Holy Family* by Pompeo

Anton Van Dyck (Antwerp 1599 - London 1641), *Portrait of the Brothers de Wael*. The two brothers, both artists, were great friends of the painter. The painting was executed in Genoa, where Van Dyck arrived in 1621. He became a famous European painter because he was the most requested portrait artist of the local aristocracy.

Diego Velázquez (Seville 1599 - Madrid 1660), *Self-portrait*.
The attribution of this work to the artist is reconfirmed by recent studies. Probably it entails a lively self-portrait of the artist dressed in clothing that identifies him as a Virtuoso of the Pantheon (an association of artists). Velázquez may have painted this work during his second visit to Rome (1649-1651).

Batoni (Lucca 1708 - Rome 1787) echoes Raphaelesque classicism of the sixteenth century. The itinerary of the Picture Gallery concludes with the *Portrait of Cardinal Silvio Valenti Gonzaga*, promoter of the foundation of the Capitoline collection. Pierre Subleyras (Saint-Gilles 1699 - Rome 1749) painted the portrait.

Porcelain

In 1880 Count Francesco Cini left his collection of *"porcelain of Saxony, China, and Japan"* (in addition to furniture, paintings, and watches) to the Municipality of Rome. Before his donations, the works were housed in the Count's residence, Palazzo Altemps. The main group is composed of Saxony porcelain of Meissen (eighteenth-nineteenth centuries). Different series of this group are on display: Comedic masks, animals, the famous *Pastoral Idylls*, saints, table objects, and the original *Concert of Monkeys*. Instead, examples from the factories of Capodimonte and of Real Fabbrica Ferdinandea (1763-1806), and of Doccia (1737-1757), and the precious *biscuit* by Giovanni Volpato are Italian products. Volpato, who worked in Rome (1785-1818), was specialized in the production of small-scale replicas of famous classical sculptures (e.g., Dying Gaul, Ludovisi Ares, Barberini Faun). In 1801, the artist, together with his son Giuseppe, began manufacturing earthenware in Civita Castellana. A group with Satyr and Nymph and another with Amor and Psyche are examples of this production. In 1953, thanks to the legacy of the Marquis Paolo Mereghi, the Capitoline collection received an important series of Oriental objects in porcelain, jade, coral, stoneware, and rock crystal.

Tapestries

The series was manufactured by Michel Wauters of Antwerp toward the middle of the seventeenth century, according to the cartoons of Abraham van Diepenbeek (1596-1675), a versatile Flemish artist in contact with the followers of Pieter Paul Rubens. Later, a small animal, a heraldic symbol or an emblem, was added on the lower border. It replaced a written passage that was transferred to the top border. The six tapestries narrate the life of Semiramis, legendary queen of Babylon, famous for her beauty and her bellicose spirit.

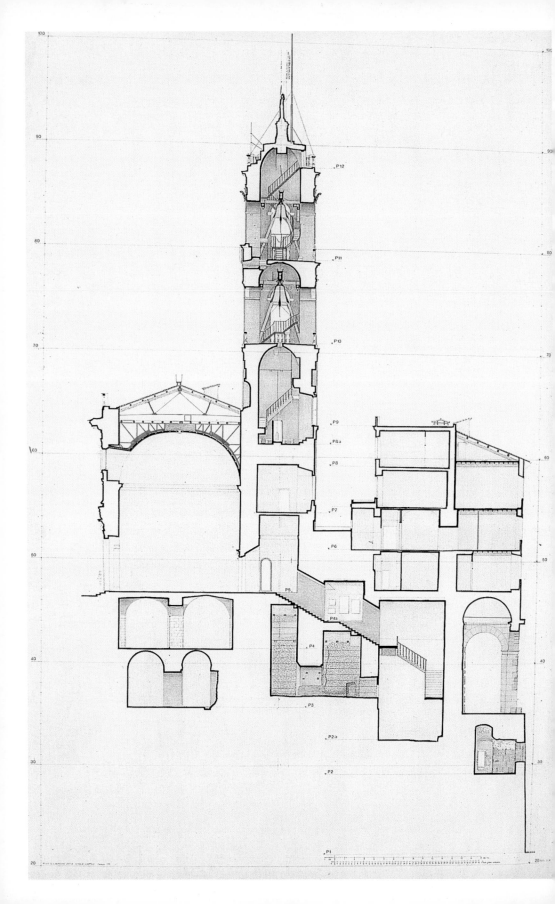

90

80

70

60

50

40

30

20

P 12

P11

P10

P 9

P 8a

P 8

P 7

P 6

P 5

P 4a

P 4

P 3

P 2/a

P 2

P 1

90

80

70

60

50

40

30

20

Floor -1

I Gallery of the *Tabularium*
II Hall of the Executioner
III Temple of Veiovis
IV Roman Staircase

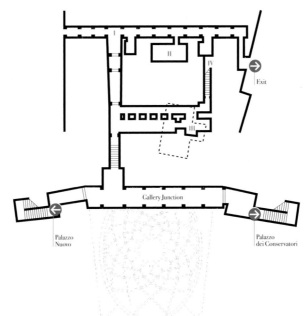

Excavations were conducted at the end of the 1930s under the Piazza of the
Capitoline Hill, between the base of the Marcus Aurelius statue and Palazzo
Senatorio in order to create a subterranean gallery that joined the three
Capitoline palaces. The intervention revealed an unexpected archaeological
situation. The area traditionally was identified as the *Asylum*, where Romulus
gathered refugees from nearby villages to populate the new city.
Currently, the level of the piazza is around eight meters above the ancient street
level. Originating from the Campus Martius, the ancient street extended along
the bottom of a narrow valley, located between the two slopes of the *Arx* and the
Capitolium. Brick buildings in the imperial age flanked the road. Pilasters
with consoles for supporting balconies characterized the last building.
In addition, the slope of the *Arx* was covered by brick structures related
to multi-storied buildings flanking a road located above the road in the low valley
and directed toward the summit of the *Arx*. Imposing retaining walls
were constructed out of large tufa blocks to buttress the slopes.
The road originating in the Campus Martius ought to have turned toward
the *Capitolium*, flanking the Temple of Veiovis and the *Tabularium*.

In the first century BC, an imposing structure in ashlar masonry and cement was constructed on the inclines of the Capitoline Hill that slope down toward the Roman Forum. The building was the site of the *Tabularium*, the ancient Roman archive. Despite the size and the importance of the construction, this building is not recorded in the literary sources. Direct analysis of the remaining structures provides the only information about the building. Interpretation is difficult because the building remained always in use. In the Roman period, maybe Flavian-Trajanic, the *Tabularium* underwent a thorough resystematization. At this time, a hydraulic conduit was installed in the lower gallery, and the staircase leading toward the Forum was abandoned.

Simultaneously, a masonry vault was inserted in the Temple of Veiovis. In the periods following the Roman era, it seems that predators and quarrymen did not destroy the building. In fact, they destroyed other buildings on the hill, whereas the *Tabularium* was inhabited and fortified. Later the Palazzo Senatorio was built on top of it. This palace was the meeting place of the Roman Senate, constituted in 1144, and residence of its symbolic leader, the Senator. The Palazzo Senatorio was enlarged and modified during the course of following centuries. Various rooms dating to the Roman period were used in different ways according to necessity. Until the seventeenth century, they housed the "salara of the Capitoline Hill," kitchens, stables, services for the Senator, and prisons for those awaiting judgment of the senatorial tribunal.

The rediscovery of the Roman monument began in the nineteenth century, first through the excavations of the Roman Forum (that brought to light the Temple of Vespasian and Titus and the Temple of Concordia at the foot of the *Tabularium*), then through the excavations of its internal environment. Extensive adaptations of the building were executed according to new administrative needs during the middle of the nineteenth century.

This restructuring took place after the general transformation of the jurisdiction and bureaucratic structure of the Municipality of Rome (in particular, after the suppression of the senatorial tribunal and related prisons). In addition, offices were constructed on the upper floors. Currently, they are separated entirely from the area relevant to the Roman monument. The gallery of Sixtus IV, which could be reached solely from the gallery facing the Forum, was part of the Roman monument.

The Palazzo Senatorio in a
drawing by Etienne Dupérac,
datable around 1563. In the
background, the only arcade
of the *Tabularium* that
remained open and accessible
to the Roman Forum, as an
entrance to the "salara"

The Palazzo Senatorio
at the beginning
of the nineteenth century
in a drawing by Filippo Juvarra

Reconstructed section
of the *Tabularium*
by Constant Moyaux, 1867

Palazzo Senatorio
in the nineteenth century
in a watercolor
by Constant Moyaux

The desire to validate the Roman monument and to connect the three Capitoline buildings with an underground gallery led to thorough resystematization interventions at the end of the 1930s. Such efforts saw to the opening of two arcades of the gallery facing the Forum and the discovery of the Temple of Veiovis in the gallery of Sixtus IV. In the last twenty years, the alarm caused by the continual degradation of the ancient walls and the danger of the collapse of the entire building generated many studies on the building. The results of these studies contributed to the creation of a restoration project that was part of the larger restoration of the entire Palazzo Senatorio complex.

The *Tabularium* derives its name from bronze *tabulae*. Laws and official acts were engraved on these tablets. The building was identified at the beginning of the fifteenth century according to an inscription read by Poggio Bracciolini and later lost. The inscription, very ruined and written in ancient characters, was visible near the "salara" of the Capitoline Hill, inside the Palazzo Senatorio. The inscription recorded that Quintus Lutatius Catulus conducted an inspection of the *substructio* and the *Tabularium* during his consulate in 78 BC.

In the nineteenth century, Canina found a similar inscription engraved on some tufa blocks relevant to a flat arch, which he transferred to a corridor on Via di San Pietro in Carcere. This inscription only records the inspection of 78 BC and the name of the inspector, but not the name of the building.

The construction of the *Tabularium* has been associated with the fire that destroyed the Temple of Capitoline Jupiter in 83 BC. After the fire, reconstruction of the large temple was entrusted to Quintus Lutatius Catulus. He completed his task during his censorship, in 65 BC. During these years, Lucius Cornelius, recorded in a funerary inscription, probably helped him. Indeed, Lucius was the prefect and the architect in the years of the consulship and censorship of Lutatius Catulus.

Judging from the remains of the preexisting buildings, it seems that the *Tabularium* substantially modified the slopes of the hill through the construction of a unique, solid retaining wall for this rise, clayey in nature. Thus, the bulk of the *Tabularium* is composed of foundation structures that create terracing along the slope of the hill. One could pass through the building to the Roman Forum by means of a steep staircase. The *Tabularium* had a travertine door facing the Forum. The walls, in *opus caementicium*, are covered with an external veneer of blocks arranged in alternate courses of "headers" and "stretchers" in Gabine stone and red tufa.

The arrangement of the building is very complex and difficult to understand due to the loss of the upper stories, destroyed or incorporated into later constructions, and the loss of the entire northwestern façade facing the piazza. In fact, it is probable that at least another story existed above the gallery facing the Forum. Some travertine capitals in the Forum area, at the foot of the building, probably fell from the upper story of the *Tabularium*. A poorly preserved staircase that began near the Temple of Veiovis must have led to this upper story. The original indented corner of the otherwise roughly rectangular perimeter of the *Tabularium* is another anomaly of the building. This indentation corresponds to the preexisting Temple of Veiovis.

The *Tabularium*'s southwestern side, located on the Via del Campidoglio, is a solid wall of Gabine stone constructed in ashlar masonry. It is well-preserved

Flat arch with inscription related to the inspection of 78 BC

in the area between the mediaeval towers of Boniface IX and the buttress that closes off the gallery. In the middle of the wall, two rectangular openings inserted in the wall frame a large quadrangular niche, of which only the travertine threshold was found and left visible. The openings and niche seem to lighten the imposing aspect of the solid wall through a *chiaroscuro* effect. It is possible that their presence was conditioned by preexisting structures in the area in front of the wall.

Excavations conducted on the road in the early 1980s revealed the foundations of a massive wall in Gabine stone, facing the *Tabularium* from the other side of a road. The road had been found already in the nineteenth century on account of basalt stones still *in situ*. A Republican (or pre-Republican) road predated this one. The back wall of the niche contains visible traces of use in the post-antique period. Recently, an entrance to the *Tabularium* and the large gallery was created out of the niche. The gallery looks over the Roman Forum through arcades framed by half columns of the Doric order constructed in Gabine stone and travertine capitals and architrave. Both the arcades and the ends of the gallery were closed off in later periods.

Cloister vaults covered the gallery. The only original example of the vaulting is preserved in the last bay, facing toward Via di San Pietro in Carcere. Arcades divide the gallery from a series of internal spaces, three on one side, and two on the other side of a wall constructed in Gabine stone. Wind erosion has left a very particular mark on this wall.

At the center of the wall, a modern door gives access to a space created by the foundation structures, located immediately behind the gallery. Originally, the areas created by foundation substructures were closed off on all four sides. Maybe, they were buried, at least partially. In fact, the walls are constructed in simple *opus caementicium* without any veneer. In addition, traces of cement are visible on the walls, left by the hundreds of wooden boards used for form work when pouring the cement.

Excavations conducted in the 1930s brought to light the remains of a building that preceded the *Tabularium*, maybe dating to the second half of the second century BC. A part of this building is represented by a black and white floor mosaic in a room that led to a possibly porticoed terrace through a travertine threshold. This terrace had a pavement in chipped white limestone with irregular colored stones. Excavations conducted in the early 1980s found a cistern lined with *cocciopesto* that had been destroyed by the construction of the second century BC building.

Ascending the staircase and crossing through a narrow space leads one to a catwalk, erected on the occasion of recent restoration. The walkway is located above the remains of the Temple of Veiovis.

The temple, vowed in 196 BC by the consul Lucius Furius Purpurio after his victorious battle in Cremona against the Boii Gauls, was dedicated in 192 BC. The visible structure is a reconstruction more or less contemporaneous with the *Tabularium*, with Flavian restorations. The cella is wider than it is deep and is raised on a high podium covered in a veneer of travertine panels. The cella has walls constructed out of blocks of *Grotta Oscura* tufa and a travertine threshold. The small pronaos of four columns contains an altar without inscriptions. A small staircase leads up to the pronaos. The temple is oriented to the west, towards the slope of the *Capitolium*.

In the Flavian period, a vault of cement construction, supported on brick pillars, was constructed. Colored marble and painted stucco decorated the pavement and the walls of the cella.

Near the back and left sides of the temple, a wall of red tufa is visible. It pertains to the construction of the *Tabularium*. Because the temple was so close to the *Tabularium*, the moulding of the travertine podium is incredibly well-preserved. In the mediaeval period, a ramp was constructed over the remains of the temple. Originating in the piazza, this ramp gave access to the upper floors of the Palazzo Senatorio. The palace spared the area from the quarryman's intervention. Therefore, during the excavations of the 1930s, the large cult statue of the god was found in the cella where it originally had been placed.

Turning back, one arrives again in the gallery. The space in a bay was utilized in the eighteenth century for a staircase, whose traces are visible on contemporary white plaster. The staircase united the upper floors and the lodgings of the Senator with the gallery. Thanks to a consistent fill that accumulated through the deterioration of the *Tabularium*, it was possible to exit the building towards the Forum through the near arcade, the only one that always remained open.

In the nineteenth century, two large fragments of the entablatures of the Temple of Concordia and Temple of Vespasian and Titus were inserted in the walls.

They represent the fruit of excavations conducted at the beginning of the century at the foot of the *Tabularium*. The fragment from the Temple of Concordia that corresponds to Tiberius' restoration of the building demonstrates the particular elegance and exquisiteness of the marble carvings.

The entablature fragment from the Temple of Vespasian and Titus depicts, through characteristic *chiaroscuro* and particular plasticity of the reliefs, a frieze with objects of cult and sacrificial instruments, including a bucranium, patera, cap, aspergillum, pitcher, and knife.

A background wall corresponding to the arch originally closed off the space that houses the entablature from the Temple of Vespasian and Titus. The arch was constructed in an unknown period to join the gallery facing the Forum with Sixtus IV's gallery. This connection existed until the interventions of 1939.

The cult statue of the god Veiovis, found in the excavations of 1939, was systematized in the next foundation substructure space. The statue, unfortunately headless, is over twice life size. It was carved out of a single block of white marble. The god is depicted according to a youthful iconography, nude except for the left shoulder and arm wrapped in a large mantle with wide, flat folds, extending to the ground. Similar iconography appears in bronze statuettes and some Republican coins, previously identified as the Italic deity Veiovis. The character of the god remains unclear. For some he is malevolent, for others, benevolent.

His relationship with Jupiter also remains uncertain; both have the same attributes – lightning bolt and goat – and similar names. A recent hypothesis suggests that the statue dates to the time of Sulla, and therefore, is contemporaneous with the construction of the *Tabularium*.

The final room allows a close view of the backside of the podium of the Temple of Veiovis through two openings in the wall of the *Tabularium*, made during the excavations.

Turning back toward the gallery, through an opening created for connecting architectural spaces, it is possible to observe one of the spaces of the southeast side of the *Tabularium*. Two stories high, these spaces faced an access corridor closed by a wall of partially preserved ashlar masonry. The inscription of Lutatius Catulus is visible on a flat arch of this corridor.

Through recent restoration, it was possible to recuperate the room's original pavement of white limestone chips. In addition, a large part of the original plaster

Internal staircase between
the Temple of Veiovis
and the Roman Forum

Staircase joining the gallery
of Sixtus IV, destroyed
at the end of the 1930s

that covered the tufa walls and cement vault is still visible. Similar features decorate the two rooms located to the north of this room, whereas the room to the south contains a staircase that descends toward the lower gallery.

The lower gallery extends along the side of the Roman Forum with rectangular windows facing it. A door, later destroyed, connected the building to the Forum. The Flavian period witnessed the installation of a hydraulic conduit with a "monk's hood" type of covering in the gallery. Traces of this channel remain. Then, the gallery was utilized, possibly as a warehouse. The frames of two doors pertaining to this phase are preserved.

The current pavement was made at a level lower than the original one, and the vault probably was raised. The corridor originally was smaller and particularly low.

The remains of the northwest side of the *Tabularium*, facing the piazza of the Capitoline Hill, are sparse. However, it is possible to deduce that, after the re-entrant corresponding to the Temple of Veiovis, the façade extended parallel to the southeast side.

Cult statue of Veiovis

Reconstruction
of the Temple of Veiovis

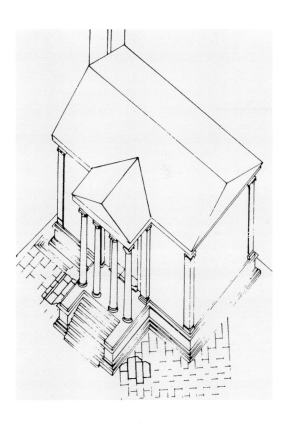

Ground Floor

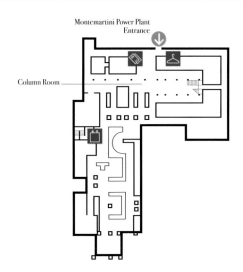

Montemartini Power Plant
Entrance

Column Room

⬙ Ticket Office

🧥 Checkroom

🛗 Elevator

First Floor

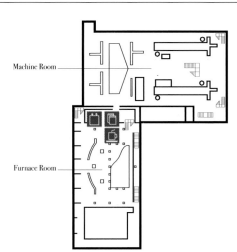

Machine Room

Furnace Room

📖 Montemartini Bookstore

☕ Montemartini Café

🛗 Elevator

The Capitoline Collections in the Montemartini Power Plant

The most recently constructed museum sectors are the Museum of the Palazzo
dei Conservatori (1876), Museo Nuovo (1925), and Braccio Nuovo (1950-1952)
Restoration efforts are still in progress regarding the ground floor rooms of the
Palazzo Caffarelli and in the former stables of the same building. Still in progress
is an even more complex project, which will enhance the importance of the Temple
of Capitoline Jupiter and its powerful, monumental structures. It will also insert
into the museum itinerary the very recent archaeological finds that relate
to the origins of the city and the oldest phases of habitation on the Capitoline Hill.
To achieve this goal, the exhibition space will increase through the covering
of the Roman Garden, located in the center of the Palazzo dei Conservatori
and Palazzo Caffarelli. This monumental glass hall will house the equestrian group
of Marcus Aurelius and some of the bronze masterpieces that Pope Sixtus IV
donated to the People of Rome in 1471, e.g., the colossal head, hand, and globe
of the bronze statue of Constantine. From the beginning, the complexity
of the restructuring endeavors in these museum sectors brought about the creation
of a temporary "migration" of the archaeological collections from the Capitoline
Hill to a new exhibition space. Indeed, it would have been unthinkable to relegate
to a warehouse the many sculptures of priceless artistic value and importance
for the history and topography of the ancient city.
Works included the decorative complexes found during the nineteenth century
interventions that created the new quarters of Rome as Capital (on the Esquiline,
Quirinal, and Viminal). They also contained the great discoveries from the years
1930-1935 that came to light during the isolation of the Capitoline Hill
and the archaeological zone surrounding the Theater of Marcellus, the area
of Largo Argentina, and the construction of the Via dei Fori Imperiali. For this
reason, in 1997, a semi-permanent exhibition was established at the Montemartini
Electric Power Plant, on Via Ostiense a little beyond Cestius' Pyramid and Porta
San Paolo. It displays the monumental development of the city from the reign
of Servius Tullius until the late-antique period. The history of the Capitoline
Museums and the history of the first public plant constructed for the production
of electricity are juxtaposed in a singular context of remembrance of the past
and recuperation of an industrial tradition.

Montemartini Power Plant

The thermoelectric plant derives its name from Giovanni Montemartini,
the Technology Assessor. At the end of the nineteenth century and beginning
of twentieth century, within the Committee of Ernesto Nathan, he prepared
a technical and political project that considered the municipalization and
decentralization of services in the heart of the industrial quarter on the Ostiense.
In 1912, the plant was erected on the left bank of the Tiber in an area comprising
almost 20,000 square meters. The site was chosen because it was located outside
the city limits. Therefore, it was not subject to city taxes on fuel. In addition,
because it was located nearby the river, it had a continuous supply of water
for the operation of the plants and machinery. The electrical energy produced
lighting for more than fifty percent of the streets and squares of the city.
In the 1930s, with the enlargement of the plant and the substitution with
the Diesel engines produced by the Tosi firm, production increased from 4,000
to 11,000 kilowatts, in order to adapt to new public and private use. Soon after
the Second World War, a large space was created to house three furnaces
that produced up to 60 tons of steam per hour. A few years later, the historic plant
lost its former role of primary importance because it was overburdened
by maintenance costs that had become too high due to its large size.
New production plants began to satisfy the multiple requests of a city in full
economic growth. The Montemartini power plant fell into disuse.
In the 1980s, recuperation of the industrial complex began. In 1996, work was
completed on the conversion of the plant into exhibition spaces. Acea, the
municipal firm for electrical energy and water, placed at the city's disposal the
monumental spaces in order to house the collections of the Capitoline Museums.
The conversion of the electrical plant into the second site of the Capitoline
Museums is in line with the philosophy of recuperating old industrial complexes
in order to requalify the Ostiense quarter, destined to become an important
cultural center. Together with the Slaughterhouse and the India Theater
(located in the Mira Lanza factory to amplify the Theater of Rome's productions),
restoration of the General Markets and the acquisition of the area occupied
by the gasometers will bring to completion the requalification project of the
quarter. In addition, there will be new structures for the Terza Università

and the fulfillment of the project "City of Science and Technology."
Today, commercial and production activities define the urban landscape in which
the Montemartini Power Plant is located. In one area, gasometers and industrial
complexes majestically rise, still in use and characterized by a continuous, noisy
frenzy of work. Next to this area, abandoned warehouses exist in silence.
They represent the remains of industrial archaeology that express the forgotten
charm of important enterprises from the beginning of the twentieth century.
Entering through an anonymous gate on the Via Ostiense, one "discovers"
the monumental façade of the Montemartini Power Plant, framed by two lamps
designed by Duilio Cambellotti. These lamps represent historical symbols
of the urban illumination. In addition, the ample Liberty space of the Machine
Room filled with steam turbine and colossal Diesel engines is visible.
Very delicate shapes that appear through the glass windows of the façade
are barely distinguishable through the reflection of light that creates a surprising
effect: the whiteness of the ancient marbles brightly contrasts against
the compact, gray mass of the industrial apparatus. The reality of ancient Rome
relives in extremely large spaces and joins with another reality linked to a more
recent past, still in our own memory.
The large dimensions of the power plant allowed the arrangement of monumental
architectural spaces that would not have been feasible in the rooms
of the Capitoline. An itinerary, composed of originally arranged exhibition
spaces, equally promotes an explication of the industrial plant and
the development of the ancient city. The museum offers both an explanation
of the first pages of the history of Italian production, and an explanation
of the urban growth of Rome through examples that appear on the ground
floor (Column Room), and in the two halls on the first floor
(Machine Room and Furnace Room).

Machine Room today, with two
Franco Tosi Diesel engines
of 7,500 HP, inaugurated
on April 21, 1933

Torso of a fighting figure
in front of one of the Diesel
engines in the Machine Room

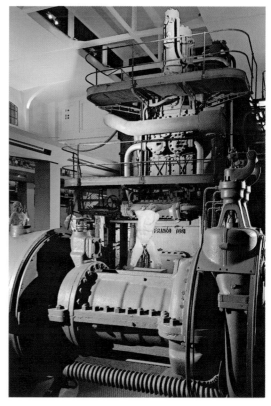

Pilasters of reinforced concrete that support the furnaces located on the floor above designate the large space. The coal slags for the furnaces were placed in hoppers, pyramid-like funnels, made in the ceiling and still visible today. Trolleys collected the byproducts of combustion. Then, the slags were carried away to be used for drainage in parks and gardens.

The exhibition begins with a reconstruction of the architectural decoration in painted terracotta of the Temple of the Forum Boarium in this room, furnished with a continual veneer to cover the pilasters and create an itinerary. This temple summarizes the characteristics of the large urban works dating to the reign of the Servius Tullius. The temple's function was very important due to its location along the Tiber where docking was easiest.

Here, a large emporium developed. It was destined to become the center of important commercial trade with populations of central Italy, as the donations of worshippers (even foreigners), found in the cult area, testify. Precious archaeological testimonies introduce the culture of the Republican age and express the climate of the great military conquests and lively campaigns of propaganda, clearly demonstrated in a fresco from a tomb on the Esquiline.

The dedication of religious buildings from the most famous generals of the late Republican age marks a change in the monumentalization of the city, as attested in some *peperino* sculptures that decorated a temple of Hercules on the Via Tiburtina. Marcus Minucius dedicated this temple in 217 BC after his victory over Hannibal.

At the end of the room is a small space, documenting sensitive social modifications that responded to the great conquests of the Greek East. Changes are recorded through the introduction in the private sphere of furniture, mosaics, and works of art. They became powerful symbols of an emerging class, always richer, due to spoils of war and military profit. Cinerary urns made out of prestigious Egyptian alabaster, beds made in bronze inlay and ivory and very refined mosaics demonstrate the owners' social status.

A long gallery of private portraits expresses the marked individualism and the desire of self-representation that characterized the crisis of the late-Republican society. Freedmen, proud of being Roman citizens

and representatives of the small middle-class, wanted to be depicted
in austere and majestic poses. The statue of the Togate Barberini
and numerous portraits and reliefs on family tombs represent examples
of this phenomenon.
The exhibit of this room terminates with the portraits of famous personages
and of the protagonists of the politics of the first century BC: Caesar,
Augustus, Agrippa, and Virgil.

Painted terracotta group from the archaic temple in the Forum Boarium
The group depicts Heracles and Athena during the introduction of the hero to Olympus. It decorated the summit of the temple roof, where the two slopes of the roof met. The work dates to the second half of the sixth century BC and pertains to the second building phase of the temple.

Small ivory plaque in the form of a young lion
This work comes from a votive deposit found in the vicinity of the temple of the Forum Boarium, together with Greek and Etruscan ceramics and some small, miniature vases of local production. These *ex voto* offer a panorama relative to the origins and social status of the worshippers who visited the temple in the sixth century BC. The small plaque is particularly important. It is inscribed in Etruscan (*Araz Silqetenas Spurianas*), relating to a person whose family seems attested to in Tarquinia. Perhaps he was originally from the Phoenician city of *Sulcis*, as the family name *Silqetenas* suggests. The plaque is interpreted as a pass exchanged as a tangible sign of mutual hospitality.

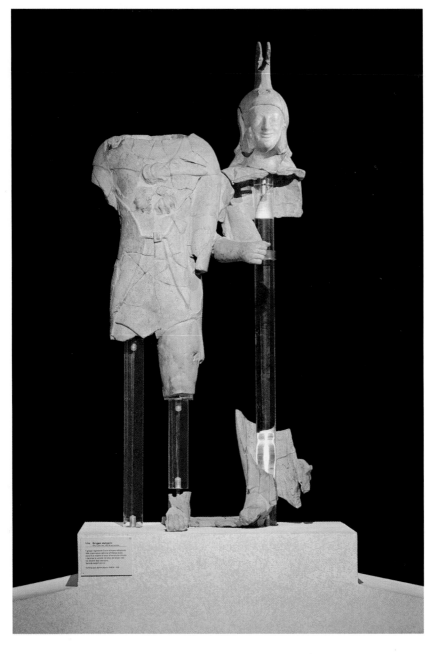

Fresco from a tomb on the Esquiline
The military enterprises of the deceased are narrated on four registers. Maybe they are related to an episode of the Samnite wars of the first half of the third century BC. Quintus Fabius and Marcus Fannius were the protagonists of the wars, and they are depicted in the central area of the fresco. The fresco reproduces motifs of triumphal paintings carried in the triumphal procession in Rome behind the victorious general. Together with the spoils of war that were carried to the Temple of Capitoline Jupiter, the triumphal paintings illustrated, in continuous narrative, the military exploits. Fabius Pictor, between the end of the fourth and beginning of the third century BC, was the master of this artistic genre. This artist, and possibly the owner of the tomb, belonged to the powerful aristocratic family of the Fabii.

Peperino *statue of a female figure nursing a baby with another baby pressed against her garments*

The figure, together with the heads of a barbarian and two male figures with a strongly pathetic expression, belonged to the decoration of a religious building, maybe the Temple of Hercules on the Via Tiburtina. The base of a donation dedicated by Marcus Minucius in 217 BC after his victory over Hannibal is related to this temple. The female figure that recalls the pose of a wet nurse has been identified as a barbarian inserted in a more complex battle scene, that evoked a great Roman victory, possibly Marcus Minucius'.

Bronze bed from a tomb in Amiterno
It imitates the sumptuous parade couches
of the Hellenistic kings. The shape
is elegant and very refined, and the inlay
decoration has insertions of small silver
and copper foil. The vegetal theme and
depictions of Dionysus and his followers
suggest the passage into the other world
depicted through inebriation from
wine and the Dionysiac pleasures. It can
be dated between the end of the first
century BC and the beginning of the first
century AD.

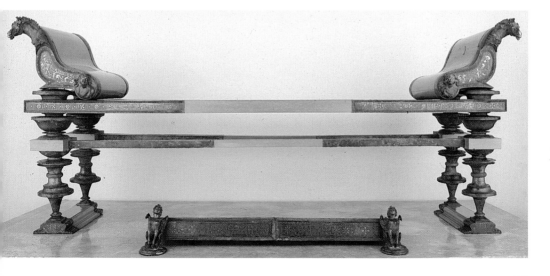

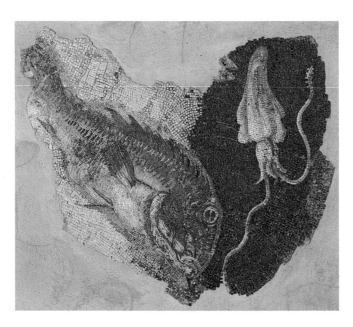

Togate Barberini

The image recalls an ancient tradition reserved for patrician families. Only they had the privilege to commission wax portraits of ancestors, preserving them at home, and carrying them in procession during public and private ceremonies. In order to create a genealogical tree, the person who commissioned the statue wanted to be depicted in the act of proudly carrying the portrait of his grandfather (50-40 BC) and the portrait of his father in his left hand (20-15 BC). The head of the statue is ancient but not relevant. It was added when the statue became part of the Barberini family's collection.

Portrait of Julius Caesar
The small head, found during excavations on the Esquiline, is datable to the last years of the life of this illustrious person (50-44 BC).

Portrait of Augustus
The emperor is depicted according to an austere style composed according to classical beauty that was introduced during the first years of his reign (27-20 BC).

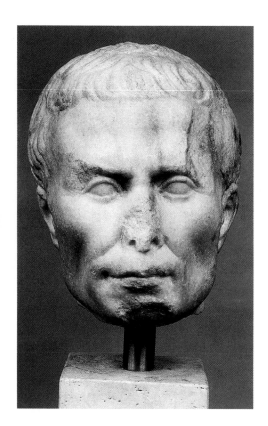

A small staircase leads from the ground floor to the most beautiful room
of the power plant, a large space divided into naves by two colossal Diesel engines
and characterized by a refined study of details. The polychrome borders
of a mosaic pavement designate the perimeter of the machines. A socle
of imitative marble decorated by festoon decorations embellishes the walls.
Very elegant blue cast-iron lamps illuminate the room. The monumental area
of the Machine Room typifies the grandiosity of ancient architectural complexes.
A gallery of deities, dominated by the massive statue of Athena, leads to the
reconstruction of the pediment of the Temple of Apollo Sosianus. The pediment
is located below the bridge crane in the most prestigious location in order
to recall the emperor Augustus' renovation works of the city and the restoration
of religious buildings. During that period, 82 temples were restored and rebuilt.
Behind the pediment, the background wall of a delimited space has a large glass
window that permits a view of the contours of unused industrial warehouses.
The enclosed space ideally invites the visitor to "enter" the temple. Inside are
the large upper frieze that depicts scenes from the triple triumph of Augustus
and a reconstruction of one of the aedicules that decorated the lower order.
On the other side of the room, some of the most evocative complexes from
the Capitoline Hill are reconstructed, in particular, monuments located
in the vicinity of the Temple of Capitoline Jupiter and *Fides Publica*, the deity
that watched over international treaties. (There are colossal heads pertaining
to cult statues, the so-called monument of Bocchus, king of Mauretania,
and the monument of the Asian kings.) There are important examples
of the late-Republican period, among which many refer to Sulla and his important
propagandistic efforts on the Capitoline Hill (e.g., statue of Aristogeiton).
On the opposite side, beyond the monumental remains of the Temple of Apollo
Sosianus, are the colossal head, arm, and feet of Fortuna that constituted the cult
statue of Temple B in Largo Argentina. The statue of Agrippina the Younger
is particularly interesting.
She is depicted in the guise of a priestess, and the statue probably pertained
to decoration of the cella of the Temple of Divine Claudius on the Caelian hill.
It must have been part of a unitary project constructed after the death
of Claudius to express the political regime and the advent to power of Claudius'
wife Agrippina and Nero, Agrippina's son from a previous marriage.

Reconstruction of an aedicule
pertaining to the internal
decoration of the Temple
of Apollo Sosianus

*Pedimental decoration of the Temple
of Apollo Sosianus*
The scene depicts the ninth labor of
Heracles in the battle scene between
Greeks and Amazons. King Eurystheus,
in order to satisfy the wish of his daughter
Admete, ordered the hero to acquire
the girdle of the queen of the Amazons,
Hippolyte. Her father Ares had given
the girdle to her. Heracles, accompanied
by the Athenian hero Theseus and a group
of volunteers, departed from the island
of Paros to the land of the Amazons,
in Themiskyra, on the coast of the Black
Sea, in order to fulfill the assigned task.
In the center, Athena assists in the combat
as a protectress of the Greeks. On her left,
a Nike has placed a crown of victory on the
head of Theseus, who is in the act of
attacking an Amazon on horseback.
To the right of Athena, Heracles moves
towards Hippolyte. Behind Heracles
is a kneeling Greek warrior facing
an Amazon on horseback who is about
to attack. A fallen Greek warrior closes
the composition. The pedimental group
is a Greek work from 450–425 BC,
created in the climate of the Athenian
culture, or, at least philoAthenian
environment, as demonstrated by
the privileged role of Athena and Theseus.
Perhaps the statues previously decorated
the pediment of the Temple of Apollo
Daphnephóros in Eretria. From there,
they would have been transported to Rome
and readapted for the Temple of Apollo
Medicus near the Theater of Marcellus.
Gaius Sosius restored this temple
to celebrate the emperor Augustus.

So-called Bocchus Monument, king of Mauretania, from the Capitoline Hill
This depiction with arms and trophies recalls a great military triumph. Stylistic motifs and the use of the gray stone, perhaps African, suggest that the donation was a dedication on the Capitoline Hill. Therefore, it represents the official submission of Bocchus, king of Mauretania, to the power of Rome and, in particular, Sulla. Thus, located on the Capitoline Hill, the monument honored the great Roman general who defeated Iugurtha.

Dedication monument of Asia Minor kings to Capitoline Jupiter
Inscriptions in Latin and Greek, located along the long base of the monument, record the dedication to Capitoline Jupiter of the monument by the kings of Asia Minor. The dedication is a sign of their homage to and friendship with the People of Rome. The statues of powerful princes rested on the base according to the dedications in such a way that the monumental donation recreated a procession of people who were admitted to celebrate the very important divinity of Rome.

Cult statue of Fortuna huiusce diei from Largo Argentina
The figure was created with the acrolith technique, i.e., the body parts exposed were in marble and the rest in bronze. The head, feet, and right arm remain. The statue, over 8 meters tall, was a cult image located in the round temple in Largo Argentina. Quintus Lutatius Catulus dedicated the temple in 101 BC after his victory over the Cimbrians. The work is a product of the popular classical style and is attributable to Skopas the Younger, a Greek artist active in Rome.

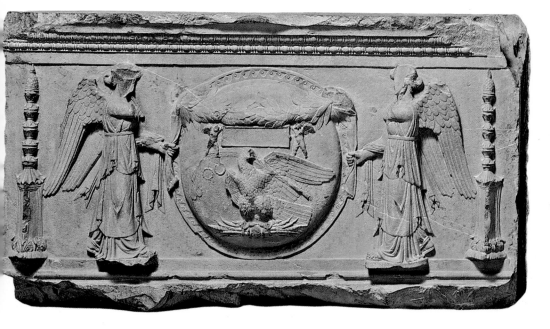

*Statue of Agrippina the Younger
as a priestess*
The pertinence of the portrait head
from Copenhagen (here reproduced
in a cast) to the figure in the Capitoline
Museums, allows the identification of the
statue as the niece and wife of Claudius.
The statue, inspired by models from
the end of the fifth - beginning of the
fourth century BC, was created in basanite,
a particularly precious sandstone from
Egypt, often used to depict members of the
imperial family. Its location on the Caelian
hill seems to secure its placement
within the decoration of the Temple
of Divine Claudius.

Of the three furnaces once housed in the room, only one remains (located toward
the back). It stands over fifteen meters high and seems a futuristic backdrop
made of little bricks, pipes, small metallic catwalks and staircases. Coal used
for combustion (stored in warehouses on the upper floors) entered the immense
machine through oscillating chutes attached to the ceiling and the furnace.
As in the Machine Room, the furnace contrasts with the display of statues here,
e.g., the sensuality of the nude Esquiline Venus, the strong modeling of the male
bodies, and the delicate carving of the fountains and decorative objects.
Through the reconstruction of the decorations of the large noble villas,
the themes illustrated in this room reflect some aspects tightly linked to the private
sphere. The *horti* are monumental expressions of public and private spheres that
represent a profound urban transformation. The development of large, private
villas that eventually encircled the monumental city center with a crown
of landscaped areas expresses the revolutionary urban reclamation, dating
between the end of the Republican age and the beginning of the Augustan age.
The villas on the Esquiline and the Quirinal exalt the importance of the owner
with an impressive array of decorations barely discernable from the outside.
Greek originals collected as precious antiquarian objects, splendid Roman
creations that imitated Greek models, very refined monumental fountains,
statues of divinities, Muses, and poets allow us to reconstruct the grandiosity
of these residences, conceived in the manner of palaces of the Hellenistic dynasts.
The residential palace is associated with landscaped pavilions, monumental
fountains, auditoriums, and little temples. Indeed, in the case of the gardens
of Caesar (later passed on to Sallustius), a garden resembles the shape of a circus
and contains propagandistic decoration that evokes the magnificence of Augustus.
The life of these new parks continuously developed throughout the imperial age,
reaching moments of great splendor even in the late-antique period,
e.g., the finds from the *Horti Liciniani*, near the Church of Santa Bibiana).
It contained statues of magistrates represented in the act of starting the circus
races and an enormous polychromatic mosaic with scenes of a boar hunt
and the capture of wild animals.

View of the Furnace Room
with the Esquiline Venus

Fountain in the form of a drinking horn from the Horti *of Maecenas on the Esquiline*
The neo-Attic work, created in the early Augustan age, is signed by the Athenian artist Pontios. It decorated the interior of the large gardens of Maecenas on the Esquiline, a vast extension originally destined as a necropolis from the beginning of the city. In the Augustan age, this zone was transformed into a landscaped zone through a radical landfill.

Head of an Amazon from the Horti *of Maecenas on the Esquiline*
Copy of an original in bronze created in 440-430 BC on the occasion of the artistic contest proposed by the city of Ephesos for the depiction of a wounded Amazon. The most famous artists of the classical period participated in the event.

Statue of fighting Hercules from the
Horti *of Maecenas on the Esquiline*
Beautiful copy in Pentelic marble
of a Greek original dating to the end
of the fourth century BC.

Statue of a kneeling Amazon from
the Horti *of Sallustius on the Quirinal*
Greek original dating to the end
of the sixth century BC, pertaining
to the decoration of the western pediment,
depicting a battle between Amazons
and Greeks, of the Temple of Apollo
Daphnephóros in Eretria.

Attic funerary stele from
the Horti Lamiani *on the Esquiline*
The Greek work, product of the Ionic
school, is datable between 500 and 490
BC. It depicts a girl holding a dove
in her right hand.

Centaur head from the Horti Lamiani *on*
the Esquiline
The stylistic similarity with the Sperlonga
group representing the blinding
of Polyphemus suggests that the statue
head was created during the reign
of Tiberius and that was inspired
by Rhodian-Pergamene models.

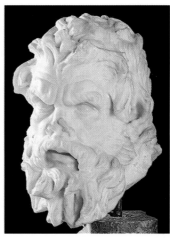

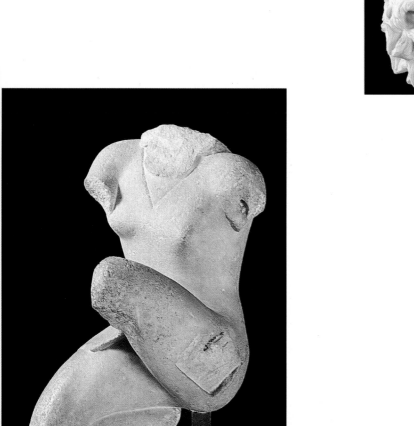

*Statue of the Esquiline Venus from
the* Horti Lamiani *on the Esquiline*
It entails an eclectic production of the early
imperial age with motifs that recall the
Severe style. The divinity is identifiable with
Aphrodite-Isis. The Hellenistic origin of the
statue is evident through the presence of the
cobra wrapped around the vase. The original
polish is still visible on the marble surface,
probably because the statue was hidden in an
underground room in antiquity, where it was
found during the excavations conducted
at the end of the nineteenth century.

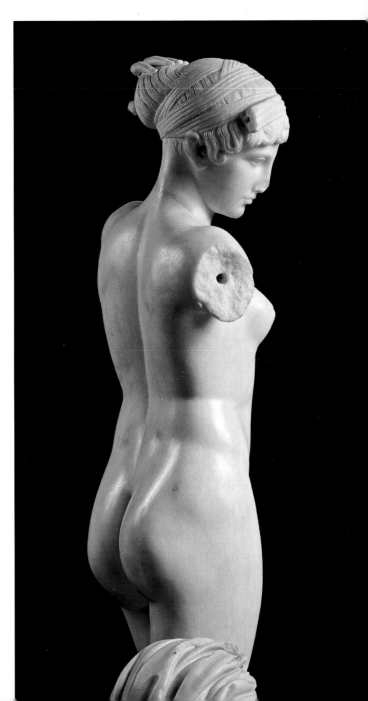

Statue of Polyhymnia
Depicted in a dreamy, pensive pose,
completely wrapped in a mantle and
leaning on a rocky spur, the young Muse
held a papyrus role, symbol of her art.
This is a splendid Roman (Antonine age)
copy of the group of Muses created
by Philiskos of Rhodes in the second
century BC. The original polish
of the work is conserved perfectly because
the statue was hidden in antiquity
in an underground tunnel.

Mosaic with hunting scenes from the
Horti Liciniani
A large mosaic pavement was found
in the area nearby the Church of Santa
Bibiana. It probably decorated a portico.
It depicts scenes related to the capture
of wild animals for the circus games
and a wild boar hunt. On a white
background interrupted by schematic
landscape elements, groups of hunters
accompanied by leashed dogs force the
prey toward traps located at the extremities
of the enclosures, bordered by nets.

Bears and gazelles have no escape. A man
crouches on top of a crate that contains
a hanging slab of prosciutto for bait. He
is ready to slam the gate shut. In contrast,
the boar hunt is bloody. The principal
figure of the composition is on horseback.
He has pierced his prey with a long spear.
The mosaic dates to the beginning of the
fourth century AD.

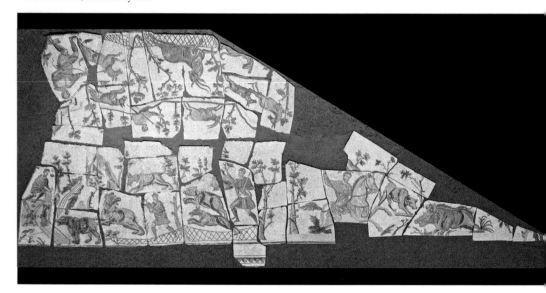

Statue of a magistrate
Dressed in a sumptuous ceremonial
garment, the figure signals the beginning
of the circus competition by raising
his right hand to throw the handkerchief.
The splendid portrait-head contains
echoes of Theodosian portraits from the
period of the end of the fourth - beginning
of the fifth century AD.

The object of the exhibition has been to illustrate, for the first time,
the recomposition of architectural complexes until now never examined together,
in order to reconstruct the ancient decorative program and the cultural
environment that created it. These criteria allowed the experimentation of some
exhibition spaces in the Montemartini Power Plant that will be reproposed,
at least in part, in the rooms of the Capitoline Hill upon the completion of the
restoration efforts there.

Relief depicting a temple,
pertaining to a large
monument datable to the reign
of the emperor Claudius

Bibliography

A. Tofanelli, *Catalogo delle sculture antiche e de' quadri esistenti nel Museo, e Gallerie di Campidoglio*, Rome 1817

P. Righetti, *Descrizione del Campidoglio*, I, Rome 1833; II, Rome 1836

A. Venturi, *La Galleria del Campidoglio*, "Archivio Storico dell'Arte", II, 1889, pp. 441-454

A. Michaelis, *Storia della collezione capitolina di antichità fino all'inaugurazione del museo* (1734), "Mitteilung des Deutschen Archäologischen Instituts. Römische Abteilung", VI, 1891, pp. 3-66

E. Rodocanachi, *Le Capitol romain antique et moderne*, Paris 1904

R. Delbrück, *Hellenistische Bauten in Latium*, I, Strassbourg 1907, pp. 23-46, tables 3-9

H. Stuart Jones, *A Catalogue of the Ancient Sculptures preserved in the Municipal Collections of Rome. The Sculptures of the Museo Capitolino*, Oxford 1912

H. Stuart Jones, *A Catalogue of the Ancient Sculptures preserved in the Municipal Collections of Rome. The Sculptures of the Palazzo dei Conservatori*, Oxford 1926

D. Mustilli, *Il Museo Mussolini*, Rome 1939

A. M. Colini, *Aedes Veiovis*, "Bull. Comm.", LXVII, 1942, pp. 5 ff.

P. Pecchiai, *Il Campidoglio nel Cinquecento sulla scorta dei documenti*, Rome 1950

C. Pietrangeli, *Nuovi lavori nella più antica pinacoteca di Roma*, "Capitolium", XXVI, 1951, pp. 59-71

R. Righetti, *Gemme e cammei delle collezioni comunali*, Rome 1955

(Various authors), *Il Campidoglio*, "Capitolium", XXXIX, 4, 1964

(Various authors), *Il colle capitolino e l'Ara Coeli*, "Capitolium", XL, 4, 1965

G. De Angelis D'Ossat, C. Pietrangeli, *Il Campidoglio di Michelangelo*, Milan 1965

W. Helbig, *Führer durch die öffentlichen Sammlungen klassischer Altertümer in Rom II*, Tübingen 1966 (4th ed.)

C. D'Onofrio, *Renovatio Romae*, Rome 1973

R. Bruno, *Pinacoteca Capitolina*, Bologna 1978

C. Pietrangeli (editor), *Guida del Campidoglio*, (Guide rionali di Roma, Rione X – Campitelli, parte II), Rome 1983 (3rd ed.)

M. Cima, E. La Rocca, (editors), *Le tranquille dimore degli dei*, exhibition catalogue (Rome 1986), Venice 1986

Da Pisanello alla nascita dei Musei Capitolini, exhibition catalogue (Rome 1988), Milan 1988

M. E. Tittoni, *La Buona Ventura del Caravaggio: note e precisazioni in margine al restauro*, "Quaderni di Palazzo Venezia", 1989, 6, pp. 179-184

G. Correale, *Identificazione di un Caravaggio*, Venice 1990

Il tesoro di via Alessandrina, exhibition catalogue (Rome 1990), Rome 1990

Il Campidoglio e Sisto V, exhibition catalogue (Rome 1991), Rome 1991

Guercino e le collezioni capitoline, exhibition catalogue, Rome 1991

Ch. Reusser, *Der Fidestempel auf dem Kapitol in Rom und seine Ausstattung*, Rome 1993

J. Bentini (editor), *Quadri rinomatissimi: il collezionismo dei Pio di Savoia*, Modena 1994

(Various authors), *La facciata del Palazzo Senatorio in Campidoglio. Momenti di storia urbana in Roma*, Pisa 1994

A. Mura Sommella, *Contributo allo studio del Tabularium attraverso l'analisi di alcuni documenti iconografici e d'archivio relativi al Palazzo Senatorio*, "Palladio", n.s. VII, 14, 1994, pp. 45-54

La natura morta al tempo di Caravaggio, exhibition catalogue (Rome 1995-1996), Naples 1995

(Various authors), *La facciata del Palazzo Senatorio in Campidoglio. Momenti di un grande restauro a Roma*, Pisa 1995

E. La Rocca, *Prima del Palazzo Senatorio: i monumenti inter duos lucos*, in (Various authors), *La facciata del Palazzo Senatorio in Campidoglio. Momenti di un grande restauro a Roma*, (previously cited work), pp. 3 ff.

(Various authors), *Il Palazzo dei Conservatori e il Palazzo Nuovo in Campidoglio. Momenti di storia urbana in Roma*, Pisa 1996

Classicismo e natura – La lezione di Domenichino, exhibition catalogue (Rome 1996-1997), Milan 1996

(Various authors), *Il Palazzo dei Conservatori e il Palazzo Nuovo in Campidoglio. Momenti di un grande restauro a Roma*, Pisa 1997

Pietro da Cortona, il meccanismo della forma, exhibition catalogue (Rome 1997-1998) Milan 1997

Il Seicento a Roma – Da Caravaggio a Salvator Rosa, exhibition catalogue (Milan 1999), Milan 1999

Caravaggio's "St. John" & Masterpieces from the Capitoline Museums in Rome, exhibition catalogue (Hartford-Toronto 1999) Hartford 1999

M. Bertoletti, M. Cima, E. Talamo (editors), *Sculptures of Ancient Rome. The Collections of the Capitoline Museums at the Montemartini Power Plant*, Rome 1999 (2nd ed.)

E. Tittoni, *Pinacoteca Capitolina ...icamente nuova*, "Capitolium ...ennio", III, 1999, 11-12, pp. 67 ff.

Tipografica La Piramide (Rome)
printed this volume for Elemond S.p.A.
in the month of September
of the year 2000